South Yorkshire Mining Disasters

Volume One
The Nineteenth Century

To George

Best wishes

Brian Elliott

This image from the Illustrated London News *shows typical pit-head scenes following a nineteenth century mine disaster.* ILN/Wharncliffe Books

South Yorkshire Mining Disasters

Volume One
The Nineteenth Century

BRIAN ELLIOTT

MINING HERITAGE
SERIES

Wharncliffe Books

First published in Great Britain in 2006 by
Wharncliffe Books
an imprint of
Pen & Sword Books Ltd
47 Church Street
Barnsley
South Yorkshire
S70 2AS

ISBN 1 904325 64 6

A CIP catalogue record for this book is
available from the British Library.

Typeset in Palatino by
Phoenix Typesetting, Auldgirth, Dumfriesshire

Printed and bound in England by
CPI UK

Pen & Sword Books Ltd incorporates the imprints of Pen & Sword Aviation, Pen & Sword Maritime,
Pen & Sword Military, Wharncliffe Local History, Pen & Sword Select, Pen & Sword Military Classics
and Leo Cooper.

For a complete list of Pen & Sword titles please contact
PEN & SWORD BOOKS LIMITED
47 Church Street, Barnsley, South Yorkshire, S70 2AS, England
E-mail: enquiries@pen-and-sword.co.uk
Website: www.pen-and-sword.co.uk

Contents

Foreword by David Hinchliffe vii

Introduction viii

Acknowledgements xii

Part One: Children of the Dark, 1800–1842   **1**

(1) Barnby Furnace 1805 2

(2) Norcroft 1821 6

(3) Huskar 1838 9

(4) Worsbrough Park 1839 18

(5) Mount Osborne 1841 20

(6) Hopwood 1842 23

Part Two: Fiery Seams and Naked Lights, 1843–1856   **29**

(7) Darley Main 1847 30

(8) Oaks 1847 33

(9) Darley Main 1849 38

(10) Warren Vale 1851 44

(11) Elsecar Low 1852 50

(12) Lundhill 1854 52

Part Three: Upon That Fateful Morn, 1857   **59**

(13) Lundhill 1857 60

Part Four: Dickens and Crowds of Grimy Excursionists, 1858–1865   **81**

(14) Higham 1860 82

(15) Edmunds Main 1862 87

Part Five: Valley of Tears: The Oaks Explodes Again, and Again . . . 1866   **95**

(16) Oaks 1866 96

Part Six: Dull Rumblings, Loud Reports and a Deathly Plunge, 1867–1890   **129**

(17) Warren Vale 1874 130

(18) Aldwarke Main 1875 132

(19) Swaithe Main 1875 134

(20) Wharncliffe Carlton 1883 146

(21) Houghton Main 1886 150

Part Seven: Monuments, Memorials and Mementoes   **157**

Glossary of Mining Terms 169

Select bibliography 173

Index 177

Foreword

This first volume of Brian Elliott's research into the mine disasters of South Yorkshire offers a fascinating, if disturbing, insight into the grim reality of pit work in the quite recent past.

Having a West Riding coal mining ancestry going back at least 250 years, the book offers a detailed account of several of the disasters which would have affected my own forebears. Eight-year-old John Hinchliffe, who died in the 1821 Norcroft disaster, near Cawthorne, was from my family and my Great Grandfather – another child collier born near Silkstone in 1828 – would have known many of the youngsters who perished in the Huskar tragedy of 1838.

I hope that the many new insights offered by this excellent book will lead to a much greater recognition of the importance of appropriately marking all the sites of these disasters and properly commemorating those who gave their lives in the pursuit of coal.

David Hinchliffe,
MP for Wakefield 1987–2005

Introduction

Mining coal has always been a hazardous activity. This was especially so during the large-scale development of the Yorkshire coalfield during the middle decades of Victoria's reign. Many of the new deep pits exploited the lucrative but fiery seams around Barnsley. In 1847 an explosion at the Oaks colliery killed 73 men and boys and two years later 75 perished at Darley Main. The huge loss of life at Lundhill in 1857 when there were 189 fatalities was an appalling price to pay for the nation's thirst for coal. But even this terrible toll of misery was eclipsed in 1866 when the Oaks fired again, resulting in the deaths of 334 miners and 27 rescue workers. Almost a decade on, makeshift mortuaries could hardly cope with the 143 bodies recovered from Swaithe Main in 1875. Within a single generation Barnsley and nearby communities had experienced a series of sudden and catastrophic tragedies of huge proportions. Perhaps the only parallel is the death on the Somme of large numbers from the Yorkshire 'Pals' regiments on 1 July 1916.

Earlier, people living in the Barnsley area and the nation as a whole were shocked to hear about the Huskar disaster in 1838 when 26 young children were drowned following a freak summer storm in Mr Clarke's colliery at Silkstone. The owner employed girls and boys as trappers and hurriers. The youngest killed was James Birkinshaw, aged seven. Sarah Newton was eight. The average age of the 15 males and 11 females who died was 10.8. Huskar was an important factor in the establishment of the Royal Commission that investigated and reported on the employment of children and women in mines. The subsequent 1842 Mines and Collieries Act prohibited women and children under the age of 10 from working underground. During the interim period there were several notable disasters involving young boys in the Barnsley area and three girls were killed in Hopwood's pit, probably the last to do so before the new Act.

Fatal accidents as a consequence of explosions and other mishaps were not new during the nineteenth century. There are numerous recorded examples going back to at least the seventeenth century but these seldom involved more than a single casualty. Pits then were generally small, shallow and only employed a few hands. The first recorded multiple-death disaster involving an explosion of firedamp in the area we now call South Yorkshire occurred at a small pit off Genne Lane, in Worsbrough township, near Barnsley in 1755. Five men died. For the purpose of this book, the explosion at Barnby Furnace, near Cawthorne, in which seven men were killed is the first to be discussed. Another, almost forgotten accident, took place in the same area sixteen years later. At Norcroft colliery in 1821 ten miners including three eight-year-old boys met a terrible end when the winding rope snapped.

Read the local news columns of Yorkshire's Victorian newspapers and you will see that accidents involving the death of one or two miners were extremely common at this time. Far more men and boys were killed in small mining incidents than in the larger disasters. Of course every fatal accident was a 'disaster' to the bereaved family and friends. From a technical or certainly later statistical point of view a colliery disaster meant any accident of more than nine deaths. However, for the purpose of this book, several smaller accidents have been included, especially before 1850 since many of these were of historical importance.

What made the big disasters so catastrophic was their devastating impact on local communities. Almost entire sections of young and adult males were removed from streets, villages and neighbourhoods, leaving scores of widows and hundreds of dependant children. There were many cases where fathers died alongside their sons. Society could not cope with such a sudden requirement for help. Some colliery owners provided money for or towards burial and funeral costs. The new South Yorkshire Miners' Association was overwhelmed with so many urgent pleas from the widows and dependants of those members killed. For most of the nineteenth century relief was limited to the formation of a 'disaster fund' which often meant an unwieldily administration, with slow and controversial disbursements. It was only after the formation of the West Riding Miners' Permanent Relief Fund, established in the wake of the Swaithe disaster, that a more efficient and well-organised system of help became available.

For the press of the day, local and national, mining disasters were big news, reported on in great detail. Disasters sold a lot of newspapers. Eyewitness reports were used and inquest details summarised. Fatality lists were also printed but, as with all sources, care is needed in respect of interpretation. Journalists compiled and helped each other with a huge amount of oral information and, as one would expect, there were inaccuracies. Most local newspapers were weekly publications so the immediacy of reports depended very much on the disaster day in relation to copy deadline for publication. Some of the larger regional papers, however, printed two or more editions, carrying updated reports. For anyone undertaking research it is worth while checking for the availability of these. Prior to the 1850s it was major newspapers like *The Times* and, for southern Yorkshire, the regional presses in Leeds and York that provided the main (and sometimes only) information about colliery disasters. However a new and major player emerged in the form of the *Illustrated London News*, founded in 1842. The horror and carnage associated with the great colliery explosions shocked middle class families at their breakfast tables. Images and word pictures of bodies being removed from the pit amid anxious and distraught families; noble rescue and recovery attempts; scenes of mourning and massive funeral processions were all captured in graphic detail by commercially-trained artists.

The spectacular and dramatic nature of disasters of the mid Victorian period not only attracted reporters and artists from the press via the new railway system but also huge numbers of visitors. Excursionists came to Barnsley in vast numbers, many thousands of them reaching stricken pit sites within a day or two of a pit exploding. As if on an trip to the seaside one of the most famous writers of the day, Charles Dickens, came to Barnsley with some of his literary friends, no doubt aware and interested in the personal and social impact of mining disasters.

In the absence of proper regulation the process of recovery and rescue was very much an ad hoc and voluntary affair. Despite the obvious dangers, there was never a shortage of volunteers, even from men who had themselves narrowly escaped death. Another, perhaps underrated feature of the aftermath of disasters was the way in which engineers and managers from nearby collieries and more distant offices attended, providing practical help, expertise and leadership. The death of a large group of rescue workers at the Oaks colliery in 1866 did not deter an amazing act of bravery and rescue by two more volunteers shortly afterwards.

The cause of particular disasters was often stated or speculated upon in the first or second press report. The use of naked lights or even blasting by gunpowder was a common villain. Colliers often preferred to work with the relatively good light of a candle rather than the dull glow from a safety lamp. It was a choice not brought about by ignorance. The experienced miner knew all about the dangers of firedamp in both old and new workings. To see better meant better productivity which meant more pay. Some owners and managers insisted on the use of safety lamps and this instruction was set down as part of the General Rules of the colliery. Others had a more laissez faire approach, turning a blind eye to a lot of potentially dangerous activities or even blatantly allowed naked lights in so called 'safe' areas. Perhaps the most dangerous job in mid Victorian pits was that of the fire-tryer who literally tested for gas with the use of a flame. To give the 'all clear' before the start of a shift was the task of the 'bottom steward' or deputy and, as we shall see, the thoroughness and abilities of such men were by no means standardised.

A Select Committee of the House of Commons began looking into 'the nature, cause and extent of those lamentable catastrophes which have occurred in the mines of Great Britain' as early as 1835, three years before Huskar. The small number of state mines' inspectors appointed in the 1850s had an impossible task in evaluating safety in hundreds of pits as well as attending an increasing number of inquests and writing annual reports. These men were grossly overworked. It was not surprising when the health of Charles Morton, Her Majesty's inspector for Yorkshire, cracked under immense pressure at the height of the disaster era. District coroners, too, were in huge demand in mining areas, called so often to preside over everyday accidents and major disasters. In the absence of proper legislation inquest recommendations concerning safety had little impact. Although there were exceptions, irresponsible owners, bad management and bad working practices permeated the coal mining industry throughout much of the nineteenth century, with predictable outcomes. After the Oaks disaster of 1866 a spontaneous campaign, consisting principally of petitions and letters, sent from members of the public, a few MPs and the miners' associations failed to get the Government to appoint another Royal Commission. A Commons committee did interview Joseph Dickinson, the Yorkshire inspector as well as the President of the Mine Owners' Association. There was even a suggestion that the inspectorate should be doubled from twelve to twenty-four but nothing materialised. The Coal Mines Act of 1872 was a weak compromise and offered little to safeguard the ordinary pitman. It took another fifteen years for more effective legislation to appear (1887 Coal Mines Regulation Act) and a further twenty-four years for the landmark Coal Mines Act (of 1911) to become law.

That large groups of South and West Yorkshire miners became more politically active during the middle of Victoria's reign is beyond question and perfectly understandable. Together, after 1858, with the revived Miners' Associations, the miners had strength and bargaining power – but the journey to representation was by no means easy. Almost 4,000 attended a rally near Chapeltown in 1844. The reaction from the owners was either to ban their employees from union membership or face dismissal or threaten a lock-out. Some, including R. C. Clarke at Silkstone, insisted on ending strikes at all costs, including the eviction of families from tied cottages. Miners were usually forced back to work following wage cuts and disputes over pay and conditions by sheer poverty.

The writer's interest in coal mining disasters began almost forty years ago when undertaking a research project on the Oaks colliery disaster for a college/university dissertation. In 1969 it was still possible to meet, interview and correspond with a number of close descendants of the Oaks' victims and visit the site of the Old Oaks colliery. It was also possible to access a variety of public archives and material in private hands that had been little or never used before. But there is a great deal that is new in this present work which encompasses all notable nineteenth century pit disasters in one volume. It has been written as a popular rather than definitive study. More research is required on particular disasters.

The recent (2006) deaths of twelve men at the Sago mine in West Virginia, USA serves as a reminder of how dangerous coal mining can be – even in the twenty-first century. This disaster was made even more distressing to the friends and families waiting for news when a 'communication breakdown' resulted in a false statement that eleven of the men were alive and well. In China their booming economy has meant a massive demand for energy but at a considerable human cost. There are obvious parallels here with Britain a century and a half ago. Deaths in Chinese pits average about 7–8,000 a year, an incredible statistic. It has not been unusual for over 200 fatalities to take place in a single disaster. The Chinese will take risks, using old and unsuitable equipment in deep-shaft coal mines with safety a low priority. In the US miners will use, for example, roof bolting machinery worth millions of dollars. In China it is more likely that the men reach up on each others' shoulders or stand on rickety platforms. The new business tycoons open up mines in order to make fortunes with little or no regard to working conditions and safety. Methane explosions are still quite common in Russian mines. Again, regions of present-day China and Russia make for a useful comparison with Victorian Yorkshire. There is no such thing as a totally safe mine.

Acknowledgements

At a time when the coal mining industry has almost gone it is more important than ever that our industrial and social history – no matter how distressing – is told. I am, therefore, extremely grateful to Charles Hewitt and all my friends and colleagues at Wharncliffe/Pen & Sword Books of Barnsley to allow me to complete the first of a two volume project on South Yorkshire coal mining disasters. Special thanks are due to Ian Winstanley and his excellent website (www.cmhrc.co.uk). I would also like to thank David Hinchliffe for writing the Foreword and for his continued encouragement. Geoffrey Howse has been an excellent companion on my recent research visits to London. I am very grateful to Gary Hawley who was kind enough to share his knowledge of mining in the Silkstone, Cawthorne and Higham areas. Mike Gill provided material courtesy of The Northern Mine Research Society. Lord Mason of Barnsley loaned me several items from his personal archive and it was great to share some of my ideas with fellow author Len Markham. Staff at the National Coal Mining Museum for England have always shown interest in my work as have friends at the National Union of Mineworkers, particularly Philip Thompson and Ken Capstick. I would also like to thank and congratulate Steve Wyatt regarding his mining medallion project. My work on local history continues to receive encouragement from Barnsley Metropolitan Council and I would like to say a particular thanks to Councillors Steve Houghton, Joe Hayward and Len Picken. Barry Crabtree of Doncaster Free Press has also been very supportive. I am also grateful to the many individuals that I have met over the years who have attended my local history classes or lectures as well as those who have discussed with me their mining interests and ancestry.

Lastly, I would like to say a special thanks to Helen Vodden at Pen & Sword Books, and to Malcolm at Phoenix for the excellent design, and to my wife, Angela.

Part One

Children of the Dark
1800–1842

'I hurry with my brother. I don't like it but my father can't keep me without going. It's hard work and it tired my back. I go down the shaft about half past five and stop a bit and then begin again..I'd rather be at school . . . I can't write.'
Matilda Carr, aged 12, Silkstone, 18 March 1841

'I have to trap without a light, and I'm scared. Sometimes I sing when I have a light, but not in the dark . . . I don't like being in the pit.'
Sarah Gooder, aged 8, Gawber, 1841

(1) Barnby Furnace Colliery

Location: Barnby Furnace, Cawthorne
Type: Explosion
Fatalities: 7
Date: Monday 19 August 1805

The earliest memorial to a significant multiple-fatality mining disaster in South Yorkshire can be seen at the north side of Cawthorne churchyard, near Barnsley. A gravestone there records the deaths 'of seven men who lost their lives at Barnby Colliery by Fire-Damp', on 19 May (August) 1805, naming them as John Teasdale, aged 37, Mark Teasdale (his elder brother, 48), William Burkit [Burkett] (33), Charles Parker (29), John Hobson (35), Joseph Parkin (21) and Vincent Hey (buried at Silkstone).

Provided by public subscription, the Barnby Furnace monument in Cawthorne churchyard is the earliest extant memorial to a mining disaster in South Yorkshire. Photo: Brian Elliott

A boy trapper (c.1840) at work. From the '1842' display at the National Mining Museum for England, Caphouse Colliery, Wakefield. Photo: Brian Elliott

In the absence of any local press, a brief report of the disaster, naming six of the victims, appeared in the *York Courant* of Monday 26 August 1805:

Charles Parker, John Teasdale, Mark Teasdale, Vincent Hey, William Burkett, and John Hobson, all lost their lives on Monday last, at Barnby Furnace Colliery, near Cawthorne, belonging Messrs. Dawson, Jarratt & Co., by the explosion of fire-damp. This dreadful calamity is increased by four of them, who had families, having left fourteen orphaned children unprovided for. Several other persons had recently fallen victims to their humanity in attempting to extricate the unfortunate sufferers.

On the same day the *Leeds Intelligencer*, probably from the same source, refers to the human tragedy of the disaster and also the inquests:

And on Wednesday inquests were held on the bodies of . . . the six colliers, who were killed by an explosion of fire-damp, on the Monday before . . . at Barnby Furnace, in the parish of Cawthorne; what adds to the affliction of this unfortunate accident is that four of them have left wives and families; and fourteen children are rendered fatherless. Verdicts – Accidental death.

Twenty-one-year-old Joseph Parkin may have been the last body recovered, since he is not mentioned in either newspaper report.

What, then, were the circumstances concerning this early and shocking disaster? A short account, under the heading THE EXPLOSION AT BARNBY FURNACE

Sir Humphrey Davy (1771–1829) who in 1815 invented a safety lamp for use in mines. Author's collection

A nineteenth century Davy-type lamp. Photo: Brian Elliott

COLLIERY appeared, albeit more than seventy years later (22 January 1876), in the 'Notes and Queries' section of the *Barnsley Chronicle*, providing Victorian readers with brief details:

> *A trap-door had been left open during the night. When the men went down in the morning they found that something was wrong. Charles Parkin and six others went down to shut it with a lighted torch. As soon as it was shut the explosion occurred. It was sometime before the bodies could be recovered.*

The closure of the trap door whilst carrying an unprotected flame in a confined area of poor ventilation may seem an incredibly foolish act; but naked lights were in common usage at this time, and the miners, some of them experienced men, would have been aware that it was a dangerous practice. The Davy and other safety lamps, even when available after c.1815 were not popular by the colliers who preferred a better working light from candles.

The *Barnsley Chronicle* account also referred to the memorial to the victims as being provided 'by public subscription'.

Barnby Furnace Colliery was established by the Low Moor Iron Company of Bradford

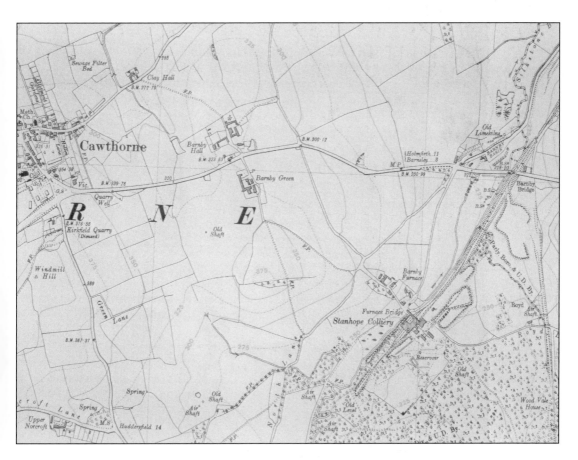

Cawthorne and Barnby Furnace in about 1920. Courtesy of the Ordnance Survey

(Jarratt and Dawson being partners at the time of the explosion) who had been granted a lease by the local landowner, Walter Spencer-Stanhope of Cannon Hall, in about 1800. The mineral-bearing Silkstone valley included the Silkstone seam, a great attraction for the Company's demand for quality coking coal. The extension of the Barnsley Canal to nearby Barnby Basin, in 1802, must have been a commercial incentive for immediate sinking to commence at Barnby Furnace, an old iron-producing area. Indeed, a tramway was laid linking pit to basin, a distance of about half a mile. The unlucky Teasdale brothers were brought to Cawthorne because of their experience in sinking deep pits in the northern coalfield (around Newcastle); the Silkstone was probably reached at about 140 yards, an exceptional depth for the locality.

Local mining engineer G H Teasdale, a direct descendant of John and Mark Teasdale, in a manuscript on the Silkstone coal and coal pits, written in 1901, states that Barnby Furnace Colliery reopened after the disaster 'but only after the men insisted on new mining practices which would result in better underground ventilation.' This probably meant widening the underground roadways (which would have been probably no more than four feet in height), a considerable task, but the colliery was abandoned soon afterwards, in about 1806 or 1807. The site and perhaps even the old Barnby shafts were used by the Wilsons' (Daniel and Thomas) mines a few years later. The later Barnby Furnace Colliery closed in 1872. Stanhope Silkstone Colliery functioned in this area from 1876–c.1928.

The original Barnby Furnace Colliery, therefore, had a short but troubled history, one that would have been remembered with great sadness by people living in and around the pleasant countryside to the west of Barnsley over several generations, and especially by relatives of the deceased. The Barnby explosion was the first of a trio of terrible pit disasters in the Cawthorne-Silkstone area, culminating with the Huskar tragedy of 1838.

(2) Norcroft Colliery

Location: Cawthorne, Barnsley
Type: Winding accident
Fatalities: 10
Date: Wednesday 23 May 1821

The grim prospect of burnt, crushed, gassed, even unrecovered bodies was a terrible and lasting experience for the bereaved families of pit disaster victims. The frantic rush to the pit-top and anxious wait for news of a loved one, followed by identification, and attendance at the inquest became an all too common living nightmare in mining communities. The grief from the disasters is hard to comprehend but winding incidents involving falls down the shaft and badly mutilated bodies must have been extremely upsetting for all concerned.

The dreadful winding accident that occurred at Norcroft Colliery, near Cawthorne on a May morning in 1821, was reported in the *Leeds Intelligencer*, five days later:

> *On Wednesday morning, a melancholy accident occurred at a colliery at Silkstone, near Barnsley. Between nine and ten o'clock, eleven men employed in that colliery, were ascending from the pits, and after nearly reaching the top, the brig gave way, and the chain breaking, the whole were unfortunately precipitated to the bottom, a depth of nearly sixty*

Descending a shaft by means of a hand operated windlass was always a dangerous activity.
Author's collection

yards. Six of them were killed and the remainder so dreadfully injured, as to leave but little hopes of their recovery. Most of the unfortunate sufferers have left families.

The report failed to mention that several of the dead were children and youths. Three brothers of the Eyre family: Benjamin, Robert and Charles were aged 10, 12 and 16 respectively. An indication of the extent of child labour was that three 8-year-olds appear also to have perished: Charles Forden, Charles Foulding and John Hinchliffe. The others were John Hanford, Richard Watson (aged 47, who was buried at Silkstone), Thomas Townend (23) and Thomas Blackburn (23, buried at Darton). Though 'dreadfully injured', Thomas Fox was the sole survivor.

A more detailed description of the accident survives in an extract from a long and somewhat rambling letter written by Jeremiah Gilbert, a local preacher, to his mother, written on 24 May, the day after the disaster. Quickly on the scene, his eyewitness account, published more than fifty years later in the 'Notes and Queries' section of the *Barnsley Chronicle*, is prologued with scripture and interspersed with religious commentary, but remains a very valuable source. In this extract Gilbert describes the grim scene above and below ground:

Yesterday morning, about eleven o'clock, the awful news reached my ears, that eleven persons, men and lads, were coming up out of a coal-pit – when the chain broke, and they immediately fell to the bottom of the pit: five were killed with the fall; one never spoke after; two others died in a few hours after they got home; and another died this morning: so that nine out of the eleven are launched out of time into a boundless eternity, since yesterday morning: and the tenth, that I saw last night, if he be living this morning, was to have one thigh set and the other cut off [here, he adds a footnote, saying that 'after lingering a fortnight' the man 'gave up the ghost'.]. *Oh! how awful was the sight; for as soon as it was discovered, there were men and women running in almost every direction, both under ground and above, to see who had fallen a prey to death's dart; – mothers and wives on the pit-bank, crying, stamping, shrieking, and wringing their hands together; and they who had neither husband nor child in the pit, partook of the general trouble.*

There was one man, a father, who was at the bottom, and going to come up with those who were killed, but was providentially prevented by a man that began to talk to him about the prayers of the church. They who first slid down the rope tell me that the sight was the

7

most awful and affecting that they ever saw in the whole of their lives; for some had broken arms, some broken thighs, and others broken legs, feet nearly twisted off, and broken backs; and having their sharp picks and working instruments with them, one had his head nearly off; and there were blood and brains mixed with their victuals. The place where they washed them had the appearance of a slaughter-house.

Gilbert took one distressed woman, whose husband had been killed, back to her home. Her two sons had had a remarkable escape, having ascended the shaft on the previous draw:

I accompanied her to her own habitation, where I saw disconsolate sons, one about the age of seventeen, and the other about twenty; but to see them cry, wring their hands together, and walk about the house in this distracted state, caused me to shed tears in great abundance. The mother said, 'twice before they have brought my husband home nearly killed; but the third time – the third time! they are about to bring him home dead in a cart!'

After the chain had broken the older brother descended the shaft by means of a rope, finding his father at the pit-bottom, barely alive and unable to speak. The man died when his son tried to move him, the scene described as 'very awful to see; some lying with their skulls open and blood rolling in torrents; some crying for mercy; and one dear lad [Eyre] singing part of a hymn.'

Gilbert also went to the building (accessed via steps 'besprinkled with blood') in Cawthorne where some of the dead were taken:

On a long table lay five that had been washed and their bodies bound together as well as they could be, all laid out, wrapped up in clean flannel, with clean caps on, and covered with white linen. The first two that I saw were two dear brothers [the Eyres], lying by the side of each other . . . I touched them all, and they were then all warm.

He also visited the badly injured third Eyre brother, who, despite horrendous injuries, had sung a hymn in the pit bottom:

. . . with his eyes black, his face swollen, his right shoulder, his arm, thigh and legs all broken . . . but this morning, May 24th, 1821, he is gone into the world of spirits.

Aspects of the funeral arrangements were also recounted:

Last night I went to Norcroft, and they were very busy with the nine coffins . . . From Norcroft I went to Cawthorne where they were just finishing the seventh grave . . . Nine of the victims are to be buried tomorrow . . . It will be a day of much crying, distress, gloom, sorrow, trembling, shrieking, and lamentation.

A sketch of Norcroft Colliery was completed by John Claud Nattes in c.1807. It may have been located near to Norcroft Farm and was one of the Cawthorne pits worked by the noted coalmaster, Samuel Thorp (d.1829) and his son, Richard, who lived at Banks Hall. The Thorps were exploiting the high-quality Silkstone seam at around 60 yards depth. A connecting line was laid to the Silkstone wagonway which had functioned from 1809.

A somewhat forgotten tragedy, overshadowed by the Huskar disaster at nearby Silkstone seventeen years later, the Norcroft event was the first major winding accident in Yorkshire and perhaps the north of England. As such it deserves more recognition.

Main picture: *Norcroft Colliery as portrayed by John Nattes c.1807.* Cawthorne Village Museum/
Brian Elliott
Inset: *This reconstruction of a horse-powered whim gin is of a similar type to the one in operation at
Norcroft Colliery and can be seen at the National Coal Mining Museum for England.* Photo: Brian
Elliott

(3) Pit: Moorend Colliery (Huskar)

Location: Silkstone Common, Barnsley
Type: Inrush of water
Fatalities: 26
Date: Wednesday 4 July 1838

One of the saddest but most significant mining disasters in Britain occurred in pleasant
countryside near the ancient village of Silkstone, following a summer flash flood. There
was a tremendous storm between about two and four in the afternoon of 4 July 1838. A
normally dry ditch was transformed into a raging torrent of water, inundating the
Huskar pit (a day-hole or drift linked underground to Moor End Colliery), trapping and
drowning twenty-six children aged between seven and seventeen. Both mines were the
property of the local squire, Robert Couldwell Clarke who resided at Noblethorpe Hall.
After retrieval, the bodies were placed in an outbuilding of Throstle Nest (or Hall) Farm
– where their faces were washed and then taken to their respective homes. Three of the

The site and environs of Moor End Colliery can be seen on this early (1850s) map. Courtesy of the Ordnance Survey

Noblethorpe Hall, the Silkstone home of the Clarke family. Author's collection

*The entrance to Nether Royds and Nabs Wood,
Silkstone Common.* Photo: Brian Elliott

*The Huskar monument, erected by the people of
Silkstone parish in 1988 to mark the 150th
anniversary of the disaster.* Photo: Brian Elliott

children came from Dodworth, three from Thurgoland and twenty from Silkstone.

In 1988, to mark the 150th anniversary of the tragedy, local people erected a memorial
in Nether Royds/Nabs Wood, near to the site of the Huskar pit. More than a thousand
people gathered to witness the moving ceremony. Flowers are still left there as a mark
of respect. The week-long commemoration included a service in All Saints Parish
Church conducted by the Bishop of Wakefield and a play, *Children of the Dark*, produced
by local teacher Mel Dyke and performed by pupils of Ardsley's Oaks School.

A large contemporary monument in the form of a four-sided obelisk, described as 'ugly' by local parson Joseph Prince in 1922, is an unmistakable feature, at the roadside edge of Silkstone churchyard, marking the mass grave and inscribed with the names of the disaster victims. The main face refers to the 'awful visitation of the Almighty' when 'the Lord sent forth his Thunder, Lightning and Hail and Rain', sending a 'sudden eruption of water into the coalpits of R.C. Clarke Esq.' A grim warning of this transitory and uncertain life follows under the legend READER REMEMBER! Again, parson Prince, well aware of the working conditions endured by the young miners, saw the monument as 'a sad commentary on the conditions of labour . . .', rather than an act of God. No one should argue with that.

When storm water started running down the Moor End Colliery shaft, the banksman at the pit top raised the alarm and shouted to those below to come out of the pit as quickly as possible. All apparently made their way to the pit bottom in anticipation of being drawn up the shaft. But the engine was unable to raise steam due to the amount of water that had suddenly entered its building. There was pandemonium below. The children became increasingly anxious as to how to get out. After some confusion, groups

Left: *The Huskar disaster memorial in Silkstone churchyard.* Photo: Brian Elliott

Below: *The Huskar disaster memorial: detail showing the names and ages of the girls.* Photo: Brian Elliott

The mortal remains of the Females are deposited in the Graves at the feet of the Males as undernamed,
1ª Grave begining at the South end,
Catharine Garnett Aged 11 Years.
Hannah Webster Aged 13 Years.
Elizabeth Carr Aged 13 Years.
Ann Moss Aged 9 Years.
2ⁿᵈ Grave,
Elizabeth Hollings Aged 15 Years.
Ellen Parker Aged 15 Years.
Hannah Taylor Aged 17 Years.
3ʳᵈ Grave,
Mary Sellors Aged 10 Years.
Elizabeth Clarkson Aged 11 Years,
She lies at the feet of her Brother James Clarkson.
Sarah Newton Aged 8 Years.
Sarah Jukes Aged 10 Years.

High Street, Silkstone in about 1905. It is likely that several of these children would have had close family links with the Huskar disaster victims. The Red Lion Inn, where the inquest was held, is just visible on the mid-right of the photograph. Chris Sharp Collection/Old Barnsley

made their way towards the adit or day-hole, a far from easy journey in the context of fear, darkness and unfamiliar roadways. Fourteen of the older children managed to find shelter in a 'slit', a narrow short-cut between passages. Above ground, near the entrance to the drift, water was building up at an alarming rate, ready to start pouring through the mouth of the pit. Two children, washed into smaller slits, escaped. Four others rushed back to the Moor End pit bottom and were hauled to safety, the engine now working again. But twenty-six of their friends who had opened the folding trap-doors near the entrance/exit of Huskar were swept downwards by an unstoppable inrush of water, hurling them against ventilation door number 2. It was a hopeless situation, they were drowned within a minute. The discovery of a tangled pile of bodies must have been the most terrible and upsetting sight imaginable for the impromptu search party of colliers who had descended via the Moor End shaft and followed the fateful underground route of the children. Each small body was carried back to the pit bottom and hoisted to the pit-top, now crowded with distraught onlookers, despite all the mud and turmoil.

The inquest took place on 5 July in the Red Lion Inn at Silkstone. Before the proceedings could start the jury were required to visit the homes of the bereaved families in order to view the bodies. It was a long and distressing task, beginning at Dodworth, then on to Thurgoland prior to arriving at Silkstone at about 7 pm. A grim village

perambulation took a further hour, the party unable to arrive at the inn until eight, where they were provided with a light supper. The business of hearing evidence was not completed until eleven o'clock the same evening. The first official accounts of the disaster emerge in the transcripts from the inquest under the district coroner, Thomas Badger, of Sheffield.

What a terrible ordeal it must have been for the young miners who had survived the disaster, giving evidence so soon after the event, and so late at night. Here are extracts from the testimonies of three of them:

> *William Batty (the banksman) shouted down the pit and told them to stop a bit, but they would not . . . and they went and met the water up the day-hole board gate. Batty did not damn or swear. He seemed to do all he could to get them out. They did not work the engine because they were without steam. It rained so hard they could not get out to fire the engine. The hailstones broke the windows of the engine-house.*

[George Mann, aged 13, a hurrier]

I was working in the Huskar pit yesterday. Elizabeth Holling, my cousin, was working in the same pit, and was drowned. As I was making my way out . . . up the day-hole . . . I was

A boy hurrier under the scrutiny of a collier and deputy. Author's collection

A female hurrier at work in a Yorkshire pit. From Tomlinson's Cyclopaedia of Useful Arts, *published in 1854.* Author's collection

met by a quantity of water . . . The water swam me down the day-hole and through a slit into another bord gate; by that means my life was saved.

[Joseph Holling, hurrier]

I was coming up the day-hole with Elizabeth Taylor and some others. We heard the water coming and me and Elizabeth got into a slit in the day-hole and we stopped there until we could get out. The water that went down the day-hole passed us. The water met the others as they were coming up . . . and drove them against the door and they drowned.

[Uriah Jubb, hurrier]

The jury returned a verdict of accidental death by drowning.

The first local historian to write in some detail about the disaster was John Hugh Burland whose 'Annals of Barnsley' was a regular feature in the *Barnsley Chronicle* during the 1870s, and therefore within living memory of many people affected by the tragedy. Here, he describes some effects of the two-hour onslaught of thunder, hail and rain:

David Johnson, William Darwent, and Joseph Redfearn had their crops totally destroyed, and John Ounsworth had seven acres destroyed. Joseph Wood, of Silkstone Common, observed, near Pinfold Hill, in the township of Thurgoland, hailstone two-inches long and an inch thick. A portion of the embankment of Stainborough dam was washed away. Ten kine [cattle] belonging to John Archer, of Saville Hall, which were grazing in the valley, were carried through the dam . . . until they arrived at Stainborough Mill and scampered home . . . Hailstones lay unthawed several days. The windows of Wentworth Castle were broken, and all the glass of the greenhouses and hothouses was smashed . . . The enormous hailstones scattered the skylights of the Castle, and the hail and rain poured into the interior like a deluge; the water rushed down the staircases with the noise and velocity of cataracts.

Burland also wrote about the main funeral scene:

Thousands assembled to witness the long procession; and truly affecting it was to behold coffin after coffin, each followed by weeping and bereaved parents and relatives. The

Looking towards All Saints' Church, Silkstone from the Huskar disaster monument. Photo: Brian Elliott

multitude looked on in solemn silence, which was only broken by audible expressions of grief which burst from the mourners . . . The bodies were deposited in seven graves; the boys in four, which were in one row . . . and the remaining grave three coffins. The girls were interred in a row of three graves at the feet of the boys . . .

The children who lost their lives on that terrible day in 1838 were:

George Burkinshaw, aged 10
Joseph Burkinshaw (brother of George), aged 7
Isaac Wright, aged 12
Abraham Wright (brother of Abraham), aged 8

James Clarkson, aged 16
Francis Hoyland, aged 13
William Atick, aged 12
Samuel Atick (brother of William, incorrectly inscribed as 'Samuel Horne' on the
    monument), aged 10
Eli Hutchinson, aged 9
George Garnett, aged 9
John Simpson, aged 9
George Lamb, aged 8
William Womersley, aged 8
James Turton, aged 10
John Gothard, aged 8
Catherine Garnet, aged 11
Hannah Webster, aged 13
Elizabeth Carr, aged 13
Ann Moss, aged 9
Elizabeth Holling, aged 15
Ellen Parker, aged 15
Hannah Taylor, aged 17
Mary Sellers, aged 10
Elizabeth Clarkson (sister of James), aged 11
Sarah Newton, aged 8
Sarah Jukes, aged 10

The average age of the children who died was only 10.8 years.

Despite the recommendations of inquests, enquiries and reports, few mining disasters have had direct and immediate impact on legislation. In this respect Huskar was exceptional. News of the tragedy shocked young Queen Victoria and was the

A lonely boy trapper opens the air door for the hurrier, a young lad probably not much older than himself. Author's collection

subject of discussion in both the London press and parliament. There is no doubt that the Huskar tragedy was a factor in the formation of the Royal Commission, established in 1840, which examined the employment of children and young persons in mines. The information collected by sub-commissioners included evidence collected from the Barnsley and Silkstone areas. What became a classic and famous report, illustrated for the benefit of busy MPs, was published in May 1842. A month later, Lord Ashley (later the Earl of Shaftsbury) introduced a Bill, modified considerably by land-owning members of the House of Lords, but passed on 4 August (and effective from 1 March 1843), prohibiting the employment of women, and children under the age of ten, from working underground in coal mines. By the end of the year the first Commissioner for Mines was appointed but with an impossible remit – given the huge geographic area he had to administer.

(4) Pit: Worsbrough Park Colliery

Location: Worsbrough, Barnsley
Type: Winding/shaft accident
Fatalities: 4
Date: Wednesday 29 May 1839

Another, barely reported, winding accident occurred, at Worsbrough Park Colliery, a short distance from old Worsbrough village, on the Edmunds estate, in the early summer of 1839. Hempen ropes were commonly used to haul workers and materials up and down the shafts and, in the absence of any official policy or General Rules, break-ages could occur. Ropes were even re-spliced to save the expense of renewal. Even in the 1830s shafts could be over 100 yards deep, therefore a plunge from top to bottom meant that there was virtually no prospect of survival. Men and boys routinely rode in shafts via an open-sided timber cage or even in a corf or basket. The 'engine-man' at the pit-bank could be a lad under the age of fifteen, the minimum age imposed only after the 1842 Act, a regulation which was not strictly adhered to. A boy of twelve could be employed as 'winder' for a few shillings a week, one of the most crucial jobs at any shaft

The capped shaft of Worsbrough Park Colliery c.1974. A.K. Clayton/Author's collection

mine. The Worsbrough Park event was particularly tragic since it involved the death of a father and two sons, who were ascending together at the end of their shift. A short account appeared in the *Leeds Intelligencer* of 1 June 1839:

> *On Wednesday afternoon a melancholy accident occurred at what is called Park-field Colliery, near Barnsley, belonging to Messrs Field, Coopers, and Company, by which four lives were lost. It appears that the poor unfortunate men were ascending the shaft, and on arriving at the top, the rope broke close by the corve, and down they fell to the bottom, a depth of 120 yards. Three of them of the name of Jagger, father and sons, were quite dead, with their limbs dreadfully broken. The other man, whose name we have not learnt, caught by the way and one of his arms was torn off. He lived but a short time after he was found. It is lamentable to add that some of them have left widows and children.*

Just three years earlier, on 12 August 1836, three men were killed in a firedamp explosion at the same colliery.

Barrow Colliery, functioning from 1875–1966, was the modern successor to the Worsbrough Park pit. It too, was the scene of a terrible winding accident, in 1907.

(5) Pit: Mount Osborne Colliery

Location: Barnsley
Type: Explosion
Fatalities: 15
Date: Monday 22 November 1841

DREADFUL FIRE-DAMP EXPLOSION AT BARNSLEY was a news heading in the 26 November 1841 edition of the *Doncaster Chronicle*:

> *The immediate neighbourhood of Barnsley was suddenly startled by an explosion of a most terrific nature taking place at about half-past six on the morning of Monday last, at what is called Mount Osborne Colliery . . . when fifteen poor unfortunate individuals, men and boys, lost their lives. The blaze was seen for several minutes raging a considerable height above the head-gearing of the pit . . . followed by a dense cloud of smoke. The news of the tragic occurrence, which shook the dwellings for a considerable distance around, spread like lightning through every part of the town, and the inhabitants . . . hurried by thousands to the fatal spot.*

Mount Osborne Colliery, located a short distance to the east of Barnsley, off Pontefract Road, worked the Barnsley Bed, at 190 yards. It was a new pit, sunk in 1837, developed by local mining entrepreneurs Richard Day and John Twibell. A twin colliery of the

A nineteenth century collier at work as depicted in the frieze at the Miners' Hall, National Union of Mineworkers' headquarters, Barnsley. Photo: Brian Elliott

same name was subsequently established by Twibell and Richard Day's son, William, sited near the Barnsley Canal at Harborough Hills and Old Mill.

Between forty and fifty men and boys were spread throughout the pit on the morning of the disaster, but most of the fatalities were found in the north workings, in an area locally known as 'Scholey's Hole'. A brave search and rescue operation took place, with special praise given to Bennett, Pitchford, Cooper, Moxon and Charles Hawcroft, the top-steward. His colleague, bottom-steward Mitchell, dragged three or four unconscious men to a safe area but 'fell from suffocation' and lost his own life. Several miners who were descending the shaft in a corve at the time of the explosion were badly affected by the blast, one of them, a boy called Walton, being 'thrown out and precipitated to the bottom, where he was dashed to atoms'. Another lad saved himself by hanging on to the chain, despite burns to his hands and face.

Again, thanks to the *Doncaster Chronicle*, we have reportage taken from eye-witnesses, describing the great anguish and panic at the pit-top, situations that were soon to become all too familiar at nearby pits:

> . . . *every time a fresh body was brought up there was a rush towards it, for the purpose, if possible, of recognising the features of their friends; the females in particular the sisters and sweethearts . . . had to be forcibly held back, to prevent them descending into the pit with the men, or throwing themselves into it. It was truly heart-rending to hear the shrieks and groans which were uttered by those persons.*

The inquest, held at Barnsley's Court House before coronor Thomas Lee, was reported in some detail in the *Leeds Intelligencer*, one of the key witnesses being Thomas Hinchliffe:

> *I was in my hole, and when he* [his brother, Charles] *was about 50 yards from me, we heard the blast, when he came to me and said 'If yond blast has fired in Scholey's hole, he is a dead man.' I asked if he had been round the works. He said he had, and had put two puncheons across Scholey's hole, to warn him of the danger . . . If Scholey had had his lamp in proper order, I think the accident would not have taken place at his hole.*

Hinchliffe, under further questioning, stated that the ventilation was in good order, but Scholey was 'a careless collier'; and pointed out that it was customary for colliers at the pit to take the lids off their lamps 'if there was no danger'.

Another witness was Oaks Colliery miner Charles Bennett who assisted with the rescue operation. When he arrived two bodies had just been got out, whereupon he descended the shaft with the top-steward, Charles Hawcroft. Bennett stated:

> . . . *we found thirteen* [bodies], *they were not all burnt. Some had their clothes on and others had not. I searched the works all over both on Monday, the day of the accident, and on the following day. I found several lamps without tops. Scholey's hole seemed fullest of fire. The was a corve, shovel, riddle, nine plates, and his dinner in the place. I don't believe the lamp lids were blown off by the explosion, because they were not damaged.*

Bennett went on to say that the miners ought to have their lamps locked, therefore not exposing the flame.

The jury's verdict was that fourteen of the men were killed 'accidentally by the explosion of fire-damp', apart from Edward Walton who was accidentally killed by falling down the shaft. No criticism was levied at the mine owners or 'managers'.

The following has been adapted from the lists in the *Leeds Intelligencer* and *Doncaster Chronicle*, though the former includes a Joseph Metcalf, aged 48, but excludes William Mitchell:

Joseph Ardson, aged 19, hurrier
Charles Crow, aged 16, hurrier

Mass funerals were an all too common occurrence in Barnsley and South Yorkshire churchyards and cemeteries during the middle and later years of Victoria's reign. Author's collection

John Deakin [or Dakin], aged 55, miner
Charles Deakin [son of John], aged 14, hurrier
Charles Hinchcliffe, jun., aged 14 [aged 11 in one report], miner
Benjamin Hinchcliffe, his brother, aged 11
James McCarthy [or McCartney], aged 22, hurrier
William Mitchell, aged 48, bottom-steward [suffocated during rescue]
James Pearce [or Pease], aged 22, coal miner
William Scholey, aged 24, miner
Charles Thompson, aged 10, hurrier
Robert Walker, aged 39, miner
Edward Walton, aged 13, hurrier [fell down shaft]
Christopher Walton, aged 22, hurrier
William Walton, 18, hurrier

As can be seen from the list, hurriers – boys and youths employed by colliers to push tubs or corves to and from the working areas – were hard hit, several of them being brothers and as young as ten and eleven years old.

The mass funeral of thirteen of the victims took place at St Mary's, Barnsley, described in the *Wakefield Journal* as 'densely crowded, 1,000 or 1,600 persons being within its walls and three or four thousand more outside, several scaling gas lamps and walls to have sight of the coffins'. The coffins were interred, together, three-deep and two in length, 'near the spot where the victims of the cholera were buried' (*Doncaster Chronicle*).

Mount Osborne, one of Barnsley's last 'urban' collieries, ceased production in 1884.

(6) Pit: Hopwood's Colliery

Location: Church Field, Barnsley
Type: Explosion
Fatalities: 4
Date: Monday 21 February 1842

By the time of the 1841 census there were about 118,000 coal miners in Britain, 2,350 of them women, some of whom worked underground, though almost certainly on less pay than the men that they 'hurried' for and assisted in various ways. We know that some Yorkshire pit owners refused to employ women but others were happy to do so, despite Huskar and the burgeoning public criticism in parliament and press.

Hopwood's Colliery or Pit was located in an area of small gardens on Church Field, close to the town centre of Barnsley, between Huddersfield Road and Hollowgate (now Victoria Road). This area

became a prime residential zone from the 1870s, one of the new streets actually named after the former pit and its owner, William Hopwood who was a former Barnsley bank clerk. The shaft was probably on a plot left vacant by the Victorian developers, on Western Street. An explosion here killed four mineworkers, including three young females. It is highly likely that there would have been much local discussion about the event, though its extent is difficult to ascertain in the absence of any Barnsley newspaper at this time. It was left to the neighbouring press to report the news. The *Doncaster Chronicle* included a short, mainly factual, account of the accident in its edition of 25 February 1842:

> *On Monday morning, betwixt the hours of six and seven o'clock, an explosion of fire damp took place at the colliery belonging to Messrs. Hopwood & Co., Barnsley, by which four persons were killed, namely three girls and one man. What makes the case doubly distressing is, two of the females whose names are Mallinder, supported their mother, who is a widow. The other girl's name is Dey, and the man generally went by the name 'Soldier Billy'.*

The Sheffield press was more forthcoming in regard to the event, the *Sheffield Iris* identifying the deceased as William Garton ('Soldier Billy', aged 22), Ann Mallinder (aged 16), Elizabeth Mallinder (aged 14) and Mary Dey (aged 15). A man called Makin was 'seriously burned' and two more 'slightly burned'. Background details, presumably obtained from a local source via eye-witnesses, were also reported:

> *The four dead persons were on their way to work about a hundred yards from the pit bottom, when the girls' candles were put out by black damp. Garton held his candle above his head where it ignited the inflammable gas. The four were found lying together, badly burned, and quite dead.*

The *Iris* also reported some of the evidence that emerged at the inquest. In order to check the depth of some underground water Thomas Farras was let down the pit the night before the explosion, and again at 6 am prior to the day-shift starting. He said that there had been 'some quarrelling' by the hurriers on the surface, arguing about who should make the first

Susan Pitchforth, aged 11, was a hurrier at Lindley Pit, Huddersfield in 1841. She gave evidence to the subsequent Children's Employment Commission report. Author's collection

descent. There was crucial testimony from the pit's steward, Martin Gomersall, who stated that he did not enter the pit himself on a daily basis in order to check that it was 'free from sulphur' (gas); but on the day he had sent Joseph Oxley (a 'dataller' or odd job man) to examine the roadways and the 'pan', the underground fire that would have been used to influence the flow of air, the pit having been free of fire damp for seven years. The workers who gave evidence stated that they used candles 'as the black damp always put out the [flames of the] safety lamps.' One witness said that he had no candle when he went down to help after the explosion; instead he carried a blazing rope to the far end of the pit 'and thought myself safe.' Gomersall was recalled and censored for 'gross neglect', prior to the usual 'accidental death' verdict.

Mrs Mallinder, the mother of two of the girls killed in the pit, whose husband had died three weeks previously, was unable to get any financial assistance, despite appeals to the Barnsley Overseer, as she resided outside St Mary's parish.

Unusually, we have a first-hand account of young women mineworkers at Hopwood since the pit was visited by 32-year-old Jellinger Symonds, one of the sub-commissioners appointed to gather information for the Royal Commission. He descended Hopwood less than a year before the disaster, on 16 March 1841. Jellinger's first impressions concerned indecency:

> On descending Messrs Hopwood's pit at Barnsley, I found assembled round a fire a group of men, boys, and girls, some of whom were the age of puberty; the girls as well as the boys stark naked down to the waist, their hair bound up with a tight cap, and trousers supported by their hips. Their sex was recognizable only by their breasts, and some little difficulty occasionally arose in pointing out to me which were girls and which were boys, and which caused a good deal of laughing and joking.

Symonds found that the young girls were employed by male coal-getters who often worked naked, stating that 'sexual vices are a common occurrence.' He also remarked

A young half-naked female pulls a corf full of coal along a low roadway. Author's collection

Women miners in the style of Wigan pit-bow lasses on display at the National Mining Museum for England, Caphouse Colliery, Wakefield. Photo: Brian Elliott

on 'the language to which the young ear is habitated', the absence of religious instruction, concluding by describing the coal-pit where females are employed as 'the picture of a nursery for juvenile vice for which you will go far and wide above ground to equal.'

Clearly, it was the moral aspects of employment which were his main concern, rather than the working conditions, but he also carried out interviews with several young female Hopwood mineworkers. Their honest responses to his questions provide us with an account of working conditions and practices which were akin to slavery. Elizabeth Day (perhaps a sister of Mary 'Dey' who was killed in the explosion) was a hurrier who had started work as a trapper, at the tender age of 8 or 9, nine years earlier:

I have to riddle and fill, and sometimes I have to fill by myself . . . I have to hurry up hill with the loaded corf. When I riddle I hold the riddle, and have to shake the slack out of it, and then I throw the rest into the corf. We always hurry in trousers . . . Generally I work naked down to the waist like the rest. I had my shift on today when I saw you, because I had to wait and was cold . . . It is very hard work for us all. It is harder work than we ought to do a deal. I have been lamed in my ancle-bone, and strained my back; it caused a great lump to rise on my ancle-bone once . . . We generally have bread and a bit of fat for dinner and some of them have a sup of beer, that's all . . . we drink the water that runs through the pit. I am not paid wages myself. The man who employs me pays my father, but I don't know how much it is.

Several other females were interviewed, including 16-year-old hurrier Ann Mallinder:

I always dress as you saw me today, naked down to the waist, and with trousers on. I work for James Martin, who is no relation; but he is the getter who employs me.

Ann Mallinder's younger sister, Betty, who aged just eleven, also said that she wore trousers and worked 'naked down to the waist'.

One wonders if the Mallinder surname should really have been 'Mallinson' – or vice versa – Ann may well have then lost her life in the pit.

Although Hopwood was not a major pit disaster it deserves to be regarded as an important rather than forgotten landmark in the history of Yorkshire and British mining: probably the last occasion that women were killed in coal pits.

Getting washed after a hard day's work. Author's collection

Part Two

Fiery Seams and Naked Lights
1843–1856

Death, by its overwhelming tide,
Hath quickly laid us side by side,
Beware, o man, prepare in time,
We were cut down in all our prime.

From an inscription on the gravestone to the men killed at Worsbrough
Park Colliery in 1847

(7) Pit: Darley Main

Location: Worsbrough Dale, Barnsley
Type: Explosion/gas emmission
Fatalities: 6
Date: Friday 29 January 1847

Several notable collieries were established in the Worsbrough Bridge and Worsbrough Dale areas of Barnsley during the early and middle years of Victoria's reign. The Dearne & Dove Canal had been an attraction for businessmen and mining engineers such as Joseph Mitchell in establising a variety of industrial concerns, stretching from the canal basin and along the picturesque valley of the Dove but it was the developing railway system which provided the great boost for the start-up and extension of new collieries, conveniently served by branch lines and numerous sidings. By 1851 the population of Worsbrough township had reached 5,378, a massive six-fold increase in fifty years. The new pits exploited, principally, the Barnsley Bed via relatively deep shafts and increasingly extensive underground workings.

Unfortunately for the workers, collieries such as Darley Main, Edmunds Main and Swaithe Main did not have good safety records. Not far away, at Hoyle Mill, was the large Oaks Colliery which probably experienced more explosions than any British coal mine, including two major disasters resulting in the loss of 439 lives.

Darley Main Colliery was developed in the mid-1830s, accessed from High Street, Worsbrough Dale. Two shafts were located next to each other, about 160 yards deep, one used for pumping and the other for winding and as a downcast. A third, more distant shaft, served as an upcast and was also used for drawing out water, from a depth of about 108 yards.

In April 1843, a small explosion injured two Darley miners, one of them fatally, therefore a fairly early indication of dangerous working conditions and/or practices. But on a black Friday in January four years later six men, including the colliery's underground steward, were killed, apparently gassed following blasting with gunpowder. The second edition of the *Sheffield & Rotherham Independent*, published on 30 January 1847, contained a report of the accident, just a day afterwards:

> *It appears, that yesterday afternoon, about two o'clock, some men who were employed in one part of the pit, fired a blast of gunpowder for the purpose of bringing down a large piece of coal. Shortly after the explosion, an alarm of fire was given . . . 500 yards from the place where the blast had been fired. The under- ground steward, George Gomersley [or Gomerson], who was at dinner at his house, a short distance from the pit, was sent for, and as many men as could be mustered at the time went with him immediately . . . for the purpose of extinguishing the flames. A large mass of coal was found on fire, and every exertion was used to stop up the driftways, or roads through which air was admitted, and to put out the fire, by throwing water on it.*

A small, impromptu gang of rescue workers spent two hours trying to check the flames but the smoke overcame their efforts. One of them, John Elstone, was badly affected by the gas-laden atmosphere but managed to make his way towards the pit-bottom, passing the steward and two or three other men who had 'sunk from suffocation'. Eight others managed to escape. A request for assistance resulted in the

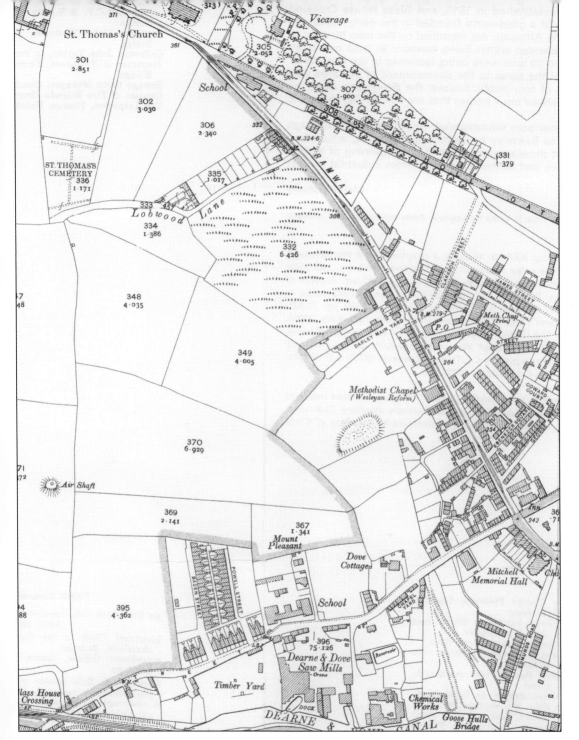

Darley Main (Colliery) Yard can be seen marked on this Edwardian map. The old muckstack is also evident. Note, also, the air shaft situated to the west of the colliery site. The Mitchell Memorial Hall was erected as a tribute to Joseph Mitchell in 1879. St Thomas's Church can be seen in the extreme north of the map. The churchyard has several extant gravestones of miners killed in disasters and is home to the Swaithe Main Memorial, erected by public subscription following the disaster of 1875. Courtesy of the Ordnance Survey

Situated at the east end of the old churchyard at St Mary's, at Worsbrough is this memorial to the six miners who were killed at Darley Main in 1842 'attempting to rescue six horses'. Photo: Brian Elliott

arrival at 4 pm of Joseph Beaumont, the steward of one of Field and Cooper's pits. Eventually, the bodies of six men were located, including John Elstone's brother, all gassed, all lifeless. It took until midnight to get them out, George Gomersley being the last to be recovered.

The victims were named as George Gomersley, underground steward, from Worsbrough Dale, aged 46; Thomas Elstone, aged 35; Thomas Broadhead, aged 50; John Jenkinson, aged 50; John Gilberthorpe, aged 20; and George Brown, aged 30, several of whom 'were married and have left wives and children to deplore their unfortunate death'.

An interesting memorial to the men is extant in St Mary's churchyard, Worsbrough but it states that they 'lost their lives by suffocation attempting to rescue six horses in the Darley Main Colliery when the coal was on fire', perhaps information that was not immediately available. On the gravestone Gomersley is inscribed as 'Gomerson' and Gilberthorpe without the last 'e'.

(8) Pit: Oaks Colliery

Location: Hoyle Mill, Barnsley
Type: Explosion
Fatalities: 73
Date: 5 March 1847

Hot on the heels of the suffocations at Darley was a landmark disaster at the Oaks Colliery, near Barnsley. With seventy-three deaths, it eclipsed all other accidents and disasters in Yorkshire and attracted considerable national interest.

Of all the pits in Yorkshire, the Oaks has had the most tragic of histories. Discharges of gas appear to have been commonplace and the workmen were, understandably, frequently in dispute with the management and owners over a range of matters, including safety issues. An explosion of firedamp killed three men there on 11 June 1845 and, on Christmas Eve in the same year, the pit fired yet again, 'flames issuing from the shaft as from a volcano'. Fortunately there were only a few men in the pit and no-one was killed.

THE GREAT ARDSLEY MAIN COLLIERY.

This is an interesting early view of the Oaks or 'Great Ardsley Main' Colliery as portrayed in the Illustrated London News *in 1847. Note the whim gin and cupola chimney.* Courtesy of Lord Mason of Barnsley

What became known as the Old Oaks Colliery and sometimes referred to as Ardsley Main, Great Ardsley Main or Ardsley Oaks was the property of Firth, Barber and Company (on land leased from Micklethwaite of Ardsley Hall) and, from 1842, worked the Barnsley Bed – originally at a depth of about 270 yards – but later, following the dip of the seam, up to 300 yards, using the longwall (or Shropshire) system of extraction. It became one of the largest mines in the county. As at Darley Main, there were two shafts, situated next to each other, but they were each only 7 ft 6 inch in diameter (more than two feet smaller than at Darley). One was a drawing shaft, used for both men and materials and the other an air shaft. An upcast or cupola shaft was also located some 450 yards to the north, measuring 10 ft 9 inches, and used for ventilation. Air passed down the two downcast shafts and, after passing through the workings and roadways came up via the upcast, the flow facilitated by an underground furnace. At least that was the theory. In practice, the geology and extensive workings meant accumulations of gas or foul air 'waiting for ignition'.

At 3 pm, on another black Friday, 5 March 1847, the pit fired with a vengeance. About ninety-five men and boys [other estimates vary] were underground at the time of the explosion. The dreadful scene at the pit-top was described, albeit more than a week later, in the *Sheffield & Rotherham Independent* of 13 March:

About three o'clock, several persons near the mouth of the pit were alarmed by a terrific explosion from the shaft, which was followed by an eruption of smoke, timber, coal, stone etc, resembling the eruption of a volcano. Two or three men were removing the corves from the pit mouth at the time.

After saying that the pit was in 'an ordinary state of safety', apart from one part where the men had to pass with caution with lights, the writer continued with his description of the scene, saying:

The explosion was so violent a character that it blew up the landing at the mouth of the pit, and shot up stones etc to the height of 30 or 40 yards.

The usual rush to the pit bank of relatives and friends took place, amid scenes of panic and crying. According to the *Sheffield & Rotherham Independent*:

About the pit mouth, and all the roads leading to the pit, were to be seen the mourning and anxious relations of the deceased or injured miners, whose lamentations were most melancholy.

The *Doncaster Chronicle* of 12 March stated that, following the fire, 'workpeople at the pit, women and children were seen running in a state of distraction.' By the time their reporter arrived there were 'hundreds' at the scene and the body of one man, George Hartley, had just been recovered. He had been working on a scaffold, repairing the air shaft that had been damaged over a year earlier, killed by falling debris that had been blasted upwards with so much force. Remarkably, his workmate, William Eyre, escaped serious injury. Three men, George Wilson, the pit manager, George Armitage, bottom steward, and fireman Joseph Littlewood volunteered to descend the 284 yard deep shaft, riding in an iron bucket and managed to bring out three more men, still alive. This heroic operation continued and a total of 24 [some reports state 26] were rescued, though several died later. Sadly, further efforts brought up 'corpses' and 'mutilated remains'; and 'carts were employed the whole of the night carrying the

The damage at the top of the Oaks shaft as featured in the Illustrated London News *in 1847.* Courtesy of Lord Mason of Barnsley

unfortunate men to their dwellings which they had left in health and spirits but a few hours before.'

Public interest was such that the *Illustrated London News* employed one or more of their artists to 'capture the scene' and a full-page report under the heading TERRIFIC EXPLOSION AND LOSS OF LIFE, NEAR BARNSLEY was published in their new, weekly magazine. A picture of the colliery appears along with an impression of the explosion and the funerals at St Mary's church. Most of the account appears to be from the same local sources used by regional newspapers, but there were empathetic comments about the Barnsley area:

> *The disaster has cast around the town of Barnsley and neighbourhood a deeper gloom than has ever been experienced. It embraces, indeed, by far the greatest sacrifice of life that has ever occurred in that locality. We believe in no colliery explosion in Yorkshire has there ever been so great a loss as at Barnsley.*

By Monday, 8 March, sixty-two bodies had been brought out of the pit, all of them dead. Great efforts were made to locate and extract the remaining fatalities, but the last three, Abraham Matthews, John Wroe and William Walton, buried under a roof fall, were not recovered until 18 March. Many of the bodies were said to be badly mutilated and 'scarcely recognisable', even 'roasted to death'.

The funeral scene at St Mary's, Barnsley – as depicted in the Illustrated London News *– following the disaster at the Oaks colliery in 1847.* Courtesy of Lord Mason of Barnsley

Forty-six of the victims of the disaster were buried at St Mary's church, Barnsley on Wednesday 10 March. The funeral procession extended for half a mile, shops closed in respect and the church bells rang dumb peals. Another thirteen bodies were interred in Ardsley churchyard, and the remainder in neighbouring parishes. Coffins for all of the deceased and funeral expenses were said to have been paid for by the colliery proprietors.

On Sunday afternoon, 14 March, an open-air religious service was conducted by Reverend Beddow near the site of the Oaks Colliery. What a momentous scene of grief it must have been since there were more than 2,000 people in attendance. One wonders how much anger was also present.

The inquest began at the White Bear Inn, Hoyle Mill, where the bodies were also viewed after recovery. G D Barker, the district deputy coroner, presided. The hearing of evidence took place at the Court House in Barnsley. The coroner and jury also visited the pit. The banksman, Joseph Northrop of Monk Bretton said that he was present when the pit exploded, saw several of the bodies being retrieved, and described the work being carried out by Eyre and Hartley in the air shaft. The coroner overruled solicitor Benjamin Marshall's question to Northrop, asking him if any of the men complained about the lack of ventilation. A fireman from the pit, W Shuttleworth, stated that, during his routine early morning inspection he did not find any 'foul air' in any of the places where the men were at work, but gas was present in the old workings, and in the 'breaks'. This, he said, was quite normal, so gave the go ahead for the men to ascend the shaft. His inspection continued during the shift, visiting 'the most dangerous places'. He could not account for the explosion. Not unexpectedly, an 'accidental death' verdict was returned, with the following recommendation of a telling but general nature:

> *The jury are also of the opinion that efficient regulations are not enforced in this district to prevent the use of naked lights in those parts of coal mines in which inflammable gas is known to exist and are further of the opinion that the recurrence of accidents, involving so large a loss of human life, demands the immediate attention of Her Majesty's Government, and would justify Parliament in passing such a code of regulations as would give greater security to persons employed in mining operations; and they further request that their verdict and sentiments be forwarded to the Secretary of State for the Home Department.*

Sir H T der la Beche (accompanied by Mr Warrington Smythe), the lone mines' officer appointed with limited powers in 1842, came to Barnsley in order to investigate the disaster. A report was published, quite quickly, on 22 March. Although no definite cause was found, the use of naked lights in waste or gob areas was condemned. Interestingly, a system of government inspection of mines was recommended, so as to ensure 'effective ventilation' and 'the proper use of lights'. It took over ten years for the inspectorate to be established. In the meantime major disasters continued.

The customary public subscription for the relief of widows and orphans was started and it was anticipated that £1,000 would be raised. By the end of the year over £2,000 had been collected.

There were twenty-five married men killed, identified as follows:

William Addy, aged 26, wife and 2 children
George Billington, 22, wife and 2 children
James Brown, 55, wife and 4 children
Richard Cook, 25, wife and child
Peter Day, 45, wife and 3 children
George Dyson, 37, wife and child
James Galloway, 26, wife and child
George Gilberthorpe, 24, wife
George Hartley, 43, 3 orphans
Robert Hessle, 31, wife and 2 children
Richard Hodgson, 32, wife and 3 children
Abraham Holland, 32, wife and 4 children
John Hough, 30, wife and 3 children
James Kelly, 43, wife
Isaac Lindley, 30, wife and 3 children
Samuel Lindley, 28, wife and 3 children
John Littlewood, 23, wife and 2 children
Abraham Matthews, 48, wife and 6 children
George Matthewman, 29, wife and 4 children
Joseph Steel, 29, wife and 2 children
Joseph Turton, 26, wife and 2 children
William Walton, 28, wife and 3 children
James Whiteley, 42, wife and 4 children

Ezra Winter, 27, 2 orphans
William Wroe, 41, wife and 4 children

The majority of the fatalities were boys and youths, several of them only ten or eleven years old:

Richard Beardshall, 18	Thomas Beardshall, 13
George Bedford, 17	Francis Birtle, 12
Thomas Brown, 18	John Buckley, 30
William Carlton, 10	Robert Chadwick, 16
James Chadwick, 14	George Clayton, 23
John Cook, 20	John Day, 15
Matthew Denton, 15	Joseph Fearnley, 20
Thomas Foundhere, 15	John Galloway, 22
John Gelder, 11	Joseph Gilberthorpe, 18
Charles, Hague, 23	John Harper, 16
George Hinchciffe, 28	John Hitchin, 15
Aaron Hobson, 26	John Jessop, 17
William Kirk, 21	James Lee, 17
Matthew Lindley, 23	Vincent Matthews, 14
Robert McLear, 19	Daniel Mellor, 19
George Parker, 13	John Peach, 17
John Riley, 10	William Rushforth, 19
George Sedgwick, 13	Edward Stanfield, 22
George Steel, 32	Charles Steel, 27
James Turton, 13	John Wainwright, 11
William Whiteley, 18	George Whiteley, 15
John Woodcock, 15	Joseph Woodcock, 13
David Woodhead, 11	William Wroe, 21
John Wroe, 15	Luke Wroe, 11

It must have been a devasting experience for families such as the Wroes and Whiteleys, where the main bread winner and two or more sons were lost.

(9) Pit: Darley Main

Location: Worsbrough Dale, Barnsley
Type: Explosion
Fatalities: 75
Date: Wednesday 24 January 1849

Poor ventilation and highly dangerous working practices continued to be the prime causes of major pit disasters. Less than two years after the Oaks fired Darley Main encountered another explosion, with an even larger loss of life. Seventy-five men and boys were killed, as were eight horses. G J Jarret of Doncaster was the main owner. About one hundred men and boys had descended the pit at the start of the day-shift, between 4 and 6 am. At about 11.20 a dense jet of smoke and coal dust shot up from

from the shaft. The aftershock from the underground blast was felt by many local residents. Hundreds of people rushed to the pit-head. The first persons to arrive at the scene of the explosion were the engine tenter, Mr Broadhead and a labourer called Armitage. Two local mining engineers, James Beaumont and G P Maddison reached the colliery within half an hour, and worked with Locke, the pit's engineer who arrived at midnight, to get the victims out.

Having received unconfirmed news of the disaster, a reporter from the *Wakefield Journal* rushed to Worsbrough Dale on Thursday morning, twenty-four hours later. The copy that he compiled for his newspaper helps us to appreciate what a terrible scene it must have been:

> *After proceeding about a mile on the road towards Darley Main Colliery we were met by rude but literal funeral processions following each other in succession . . . surrounded by frantic widows and childless parents, who had succeeded, not without some difficulty, in recognising their own kindred from among the heaps of fearfully mangled bodies from time to time sent up to the pit's mouth. On arriving at the works we found a further crowd of spectators anxiously waiting to know the fate of the missing husbands, sons, and brothers, and ever and anon the shrieks of the females indicated that some fresh sufferer's fate had been made manifest by the recognition of the body by its friends.*

The actual funerals were held at Worsbrough and Barnsley churches on Sunday 28 January. The number of mourners was said to be 'immense', and the occasion 'solemn and overpowering'.

Horse and carts take away bodies from Darley Main following the disaster of 1849. Anxious relatives rush to the pit bank. From the Illustrated London News. Courtesy of Lord Mason of Barnsley

The Masons Arms was often used for inquests following mining accidents and disasters in the Worsbrough Dale area. Photo: Brian Elliott

After talking to eyewitnesses, the reporter informed readers about the state of the bodies that had been recovered:

> *Nearly all the bodies . . . were dreadfully mutilated, and in several instances the head literally scalped, the hair burnt off . . . A more horrible scene could not be possibly conceived, and as cart loads one after another were taken away to surrounding houses, numbers of maddened and anxious parents and wives ran after the vehicles, and threw on one side the blankets in the dreadful anticipation of recognising some one dear to them.*

As with the Oaks disaster, the *Illustrated London News* ran a full-page account.

The inquest was held at the Mason's Arms, Worsbrough Dale, before the district coroner, Mr Thomas Badger, initially on the Saturday, 27 January, to view the bodies, and then to hear evidence at later dates. An extremely important aspect of the inquest was the array of experts and officials who were invited to attend by a very astute coroner. Among them were two very eminent viewers – Nicholas Wood (1795–1865) of Hetton, greatly respected for his abilities and achievements in the northern coalfield; and the highly talented mining engineer for Earl Fitzwilliam, Benjamin Biram (1804–57). Biram had tried to introduce a new safety lamp of his own design at this time, and was involved in improving underground ventilation in the Earl's collieries by means of new equipment and measuring instruments. Goodwin of Charlesworth's collieries and the consultative viewer, John Thomas Woodhouse of Ashby-de-la-Zouche also provided a weight of expert opinion. Government representation was in the form of Mr Tremenheer, the coal mines' commissioner and Warrington-Smyth, mining engineer to the Geological Survey. The concensus was that an explosion occurred in the goaf (waste area) located furthest away from the shaft, but a smaller fire had also taken place near the pit bottom, indicating two explosions. The main explosion was deemed to be one of

A Biram-type safety lamp. AKClayton/Brian Elliott

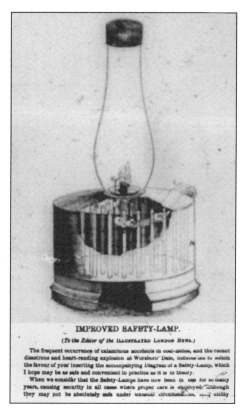

IMPROVED SAFETY-LAMP.

(To the Editor of the Illustrated London News.*)*

The frequent occurrence of calamitous accidents in coal-mines, and the recent disastrous and heart-rending explosion at Worsbro' Dale, induces me to solicit the favour of your inserting the accompanying Diagram of a Safety-Lamp, which I hope may be as safe and convenient in practice as it is in theory.

When we consider that the Safety-Lamps have now been in use for so many years, causing security in all cases where proper care is employed, although they may not be absolutely safe under unusual circumstances, their utility

This example of an 'improved' safety lamp was sent to the Illustrated London News *following the Darley Main disaster.* Courtesy of Lord Mason of Barnsley

firedamp, caused when gas was 'driven out' by a roof fall, which then came into contact with a naked light. Interestingly, several survivors [rare to have them in major disasters] gave crucial evidence to the effect that the pit's ventilation had long been 'in a very bad state', the coal being extracted irregularly and 'large holes' left where foul air accumulated, there being no air current to clear them. Thompson, the underground steward, had given the 'all clear' (that the workings were safe) on the morning of the disaster. The men were said to generally work with Davy lamps but some, on the morning of the explosion, had 'naked candles'.

Tremenheer emphasised how important it was for the Government to regulate safety in coal mines, and there was need for 'a higher standard of education for those entrusted with the management of mines.' Warrington Smyth was also of the opinion that 'a properly qualified Government' might have foreseen and corrected 'various sources of danger.' The 'Accidental Death' verdict included a strong recommendation 'to proprietors' that 'a better mode of ventilation be adopted before they commence work at the mine' and that the Government should appoint 'a scientific and practical person, to

The mass funeral at St Mary's, Worsbrough following the 1849 Darley Main disaster as portrayed in the Illustrated London News. Courtesy of Lord Mason of Barnsley

occasionally inspect the collieries in this district and see that there is proper ventilation, and hear any complaint by the workpeople employed therein.' If anything positive did emerge from this great tragedy it was the establishment of a mines inspection service a year later. Like Huskar, Darley had contributed towards national legislation.

Most (except eight) of the deceased were identified as follows:

(1) Married men
Edward Atkinson, 36, wife and two children
George Barrowclough, 36, wife and four children
John Beevors, 56, wife and two children
Charles Brook, 37, three children
David Brown, 37, wife and two children
John Burton, 26, wife
John Darwin, 36, wife
Thomas Darwin, 28, wife and two children
George Field, 32, wife and two children
Henry Firth, aged 34, wife and four children
George Guest, 41, wife and one child
Edward Hammond, 20, wife

Thomas Hammond, 39, wife and four children
Amos Harper, 37, wife and seven children
William Humpleby, 35, wife and four children
George Loy, 40, wife and five children
John Parsons senr, 48, wife
Joseph Sager, 29, wife and six children
James Seddons, 26, wife and two children
John Smith, 36, wife
John Taylor, 26, wife
George Tetley, aged 23, wife and one child
Edward Utley, 36, wife
John Winder, 31, wife and four children

(2) Single men and boys
James Ashton [Ackton?] alias 'Lancashire Jim', 17

Francis Batty, 15	Edward Billington, 24
William Billington, 11	William Brook, 14
Hugh Burkinshaw, 22	James Burkinshaw, 19
John Charlesworth, 13	Joseph Charlesworth, 14
Thomas Firth, 45	George Fisher, 23
John Gillott, 11	Thomas Gillott, 19
William Goldthorpe, 13	Samuel Goodliffe, 19
Joseph Guest, 16	William Guest, 15
Charles Hammond, 25	William Hardisty, 11
George Harper, 10	John Hartley, 25
William Hiland, 11	William Hinchcliffe, 12
Isaac Holland, 15	William Holland jnr, 11
William Hutchinson, 24	John Kaye, 18
John Loy, 15	Patrick McDonald, 19
Thomas Mooney, 15	John Parsons jnr, 20
William Parsons, 13	Edward Rennison, 18
Joseph Sells, 10	Isaac Swift, 23
Abraham Sykes, 25	John Sykes, 18
Ralph Taylor, 25	George Turner, 21
Thomas Utley, 12	George Winter, 19
Robert Winter, 28	Charles Wood, 17

Even after such a major disaster there was no compensation available for widows and their families. As we have already seen, some colliery owners bought coffins and paid funeral costs but the scale of later disasters even ruled this 'benefit' out. A relief fund for Darley widows and children was opened, soon reaching £1,300, the colliery proprietors contributing £200. Nevertheless, it is hard to imagine the hardship that these families had to endure.

The Oaks and Darley Main continued to recruit labour despite their unenviable record as 'fiery' and unsafe mines. Three men lost their lives due to an explosion in the downcast shaft at the Oaks in June 1850. A year later, during the sinking of a new shaft, Darley fired yet again, and three more miners were killed. A month later an explosion at Worsbrough Park Colliery resulted in three more fatalities. Despite the strong recommendations and warnings made at the 1849 Darley inquest, candles were still in widespread use.

(10) Pit: Warren Vale Colliery

Location: Rawmarsh
Type: Explosion
Fatalities: 52
Date: Saturday 20 December 1851

The scene of major disasters now moved to the Rotherham area. Sixty-three men and boys were at work at J J Charlesworth's Warren Vale Colliery on the last Saturday morning before Christmas day, keen to earn a little more money for the festive season. Thirty-two were directly employed by the proprietors, mainly colliers who, in turn, set on their own 'helpers', usually young lads and boys. Only eleven of the workers ultimately survived a massive explosion that rocked the entire neighbourhood.

Warren Vale was a new pit, just over a year old, sunk on land near Rawmarsh owned by G S Foljambe of Osberton, and leased by the Charlesworths as part of their considerable Yorkshire colliery empire. It had two shafts, located only a few yards from each other. The downcast reached the nine-foot seam at a depth of 127 yards; and the upcast led to workings exploiting the five-foot seam, ninety yards deep. Workings at this time were fairly extensive, several hundred yards from the pit bottom.

The blast occurred early in the morning, just before seven and woke up the entire neighbourhood. Its severity can be asertained by reference to eyewitness reports recounted in both the regional and national press. After comparing the explosion to that of a volcanic eruption, *The Times* of Monday 22 December, described the dramatic pit-head scene:

> *Smoke and flames burst from the mouth of the pit in appalling volume. Two corves which were being drawn out of the pit were projected upwards . . . and lodged in the gearing of the shaft. A great quantity of coals, stones, and other matter, which had been carried high into the air, fell in so dense a shower that the persons employed near the pit mouth were compelled to take their shelter under the platform of the tipplers for loading the carts . . . The country all round the pit was blackened to a distance of three-quarters of a mile by the descent of the dust and smoke . . . The report of the explosion was heard at a distance of three miles. The whole country round was filled with consternation . . .*

One man, said to live a couple of field distances away, received a blackened face when he came to the door of his cottage, looking as though he had just finished a shift at the pit.

The *Sheffield and Rotherham Independent*, in its edition published a week after the disaster, referred to the rescue operations:

> *As soon as possible, the pit rope was disentagled from the corves . . . and a party of courageous men from neighbouring colleries descended to the rescue of the unfortunate sufferers below. They found some sixteen or eighteen men and boys who had been enabled to reach*

the pit bottom, where they anxiously waited to be withdrawn from the noxious gas . . . some of these were in a state of insensibility and others suffering greatly from injuries . . .

The Times reported that by three in the afternoon twenty-four persons had been got out of the pit alive, and fifteen others unfortunately dead; and concern was expressed concerning at least nine of those rescued. The leaders of the rescue party included Mr Cooper, steward at a nearby colliery owned by Earl Fitzwilliam, William Goodison who worked as the Charlesworths' viewer and the pit's own manager or superintendent, Mr Sellers. After ascending the pit many of the rescuers collapsed from exhaustion and the effects of the gas. The scene at the pit-hill was, for most, very distressing:

Men, women, and children . . . rapidly assembled in agonies of fear and hope – hopes in some few cases realised, and fears dispelled; but in many cases, their hopes were blighted,

Bringing out the dead to the great distress of waiting relatives.
www.cmhrc.co.uk

45

and their worse fears confirmed. Round every body got out of the pit, gathered an anxious group; and the announcement that life still flowed sent a thrill of joy through every heart . . . Agonising shrieks from women who recognised the corpse of a husband, a brother, or a father, from who they had parted but a few short hours before in vigour of life, rent the air. 'Mourning, lamentation, and woe' prevailed on every hand.

The dead and injured were conveyed in carts to their homes, or to the Star Inn where the bodies would be viewed by the inquest jury.

By eight in the evening fire engines were pumping water into the pit to help with the restoration of the ventilation, and this activity continued throughout the weekend. The main owner, J Charlesworth, 'attended most assiduously to the sufferers and another of Earl Fitwilliam's senior colliery staff, his colliery agent, Benjamin Biram, from Wentworth, also provided assistance'.

Disasters had become great public spectacles. Despite heavy rain, hundreds of people from neighbouring villages arrived to view the pit on the Sunday when more dead bodies were extracted. The last to be brought out was Thomas Silvester, 'fire-trier' (a workman who 'tested the air' with a light in order to check all was safe, a potentially explosive job!), his body 'much mutilated' under a roof fall. *The Times* report of 23 December stated that Sylvester's body had been 'blown to pieces and scattered about the pit.' Sylvester was the first man to go down on that fateful morning, at about six, taking with him a lighted rope rather than a lamp, the pit being regarded as safe for the use of naked lights. He then gave the 'all clear'.

One of two horses in the pit at the time of the explosion escaped unhurt, the other was killed and the lucky pit cat was brought out alive.

A fire-trier or penitent, one of the most dangerous occupations in a coal mine. www.cmhrc.co.uk

Stories of remarkable feats of survival began to emerge during the course of the inquest, once again presided over by Thomas Badger. After the explosion, Joseph Cooper made his way to the pit bottom, suffering from the gas but climbed up the shaft – via the conductors – to a distance of sixty yards, where, almost overcome, he kept himself alive by placing his mouth in a crevice. He managed to seize onto the rope and 'chair' that was lowered and was hauled to safety. Another young miner, Charles Burgin, instinctively threw himself to the ground in the north level, burying his face in the slack (small coal) so as to avoid being gassed but all his workmates perished; and his brother, Thomas, in another area, was also killed. Another fortunate survivor, collier John Hague, working about 240 yards from the shaft, described his experience as follows:

> I and my son went to work on Saturday morning in the deep level. We went down at a quarter to six and began work in our usual place. We found no difference in the air ... We filled two corves, and had started to fill a third when the blast came ... the blast knocked out all the lights but one. We walked to the shaft ... with great difficulty, on account of the sulphur. There was great wailing from those who were dying ...

Coroner Badger was highly critical of colliery owners 'who ought to employ vigilant and intelligent managers, the duty of one of them every morning to go down the pit and inspect the mine, and report on its safety before any of the men are permitted to work ...'. He also stated that the colliers needed to be made 'fully acquainted with the principles and the observance upon which alone, both as to light and ventilation, the safety of the whole body of workmen depends.'

Much discussion took place concerning the cause of the explosion. Goodison suggested that it might have been due to a trapper leaving a door open, since 'at least three' of boys (aged 11 or 12) were killed. Thomas Hague thought it was a fall of roof in No. 3 benk (or bank), releasing gas where Sylvester's body was found. The latter was responsible to Thomas Kaye, the bottom steward, described as 'an old man' who could not read or write and who (incredibly) 'rarely went into the mine except to measure'. Sylvester was usually under pressure from the men waiting at the top to be given the all clear as they were always 'neck break' to get down. Charles Morton the mines' inspector, concluded that there was no regular supervision at the pit and no written rules. William Sellars, the pit's bookkeeper, stated that there were only two Davy lamps available. J C Charlesworth told the jury that 'personal management' was not possible because of the number of pits that his partnership owned, a truthful but equally damning comment.

Eventually, the inspector concluded that it was the large fall of roof in No. 3 bank which was the origin of the explosion, saying that Sylvester's subsequent inspection coincided with gas igniting via the naked candles. This opinion was also that of the other eminent colliery viewers, namely T D Jeffcock, Charles Locke and R C Webster.

After almost four hours a verdict of 'accidentally killed by an explosion of firedamp' was given for all fifty-two of the men and boys whose bodies had been identified. The jury made the point that although there was 'no legal evidence' for manslaughter, there was 'strong disapprobation of the loose manner in which the works seem to have been conducted'. Instructions to the men were also described as 'quite inadequate to their proper supervision and safety'. The colliery partnership accepted these comments as well as further recommendations regarding improved

Funeral scenes such as this were common occurrences in Barnsley and South Yorkshire mining areas during the Victorian period. Barnsley had numerous shops specialising in mourning attire.
www.cmhrc.co.uk

ventilation. As we shall see, another disaster occured at Warren Vale twenty-three years later.

What a terrible and unforgettable Christmas it must have been. The funerals and interments of forty-one of the deceased took place on Tuesday 23 December in Rawmarsh churchyard (with nine others buried the next day, in neighbouring parishes):

In every part, busy workmen were engaged in turning over the green sod, constructing 'strong houses' for the numerous dead. Some one or two graves were huge pits each formed to receive several occupants. But for the gloomy spectators, the churchyard, with this throng of men weilding the pick axe and spade, would have looked more like the works of a railway in course of formation, than a small village burial ground. Around the Star Inn were gathered at an early hour groups of disconsolate relatives . . . in two chambers over the stables . . . presented the appalling spectacle of 43 human corpses lying side by side in grim array, attired with one or two exceptions, in the tattered working dress, and in the precise state in which they had been brought out of the fatal pit . . . Each coffin . . . was carried from the chamber into the yard, whence it was removed either direct to the church-yard, on the shoulders of men, or in covered vehicles . . . The village streets were one continued scene of funeral procession throughout the afternoon. The singing of a slow and solemn dirge..was deeply impressive.

As usual, the fatality list includes several fathers and sons:

John Purseglove, 41, Rawmarsh
James Purseglove, 14
Henry Purseglove, 12 (sons of the above)
John Hartley, 31, Rawmarsh
John Walton, jnr, (14), Rawmarsh
William Froggatt, 12, Rawmarsh
William Garnett alias Whyke, 41, Rawmarsh
John Siddons, 21, Lee Brook, nr Wentworth
James Johnson, 15, Lane Head
William Schofield, 26, Lane Head
Thomas Sylvester, jnr, 19, Thorpe
George Sellers, 11, Pinch Row, Swinton
(his father, Jonathan much injured and in Sheffield Infirmary)
George Hague, 32, Rawmarsh
James Shepherd, 21, Rawmarsh
Thomas Taylor, 27, Upper Haugh
George Robinson, 23, Rawmarsh
Benjamin Walker, 55, Rawmarsh
Samuel Siddons, 29, Rawmarsh
William Cooper, 31, Rawmarsh
Henry Goddard, 30, Thorpe
John Thompson, 31, Rawmarsh
James Roberts, 16
Joseph Roberts, jnr, 16 (sons of Joseph Roberts, labourer)
Abraham Cooper, 41, Kilnhurst
John Cooper, 16 (son of above)
Thomas Burgin, Rawmarsh
Joseph Bugg, 40, Lane Head
Benjamin Lane, Rawmarsh
Henry James, 36, Mount Pleasant, Wath
Charles Cousins, 35, Pinch Row, Swinton
George Cousins, 11 (son of the above)
Thomas Johnson, 31, Rawmarsh
Henry Thompson, 27, Thorpe
William Ashton, 18, Rawmarsh
Henry Ward, 26, Rawmarsh
Thomas Farmery, 20, Upper Haugh
Henry Lee, 27, Upper Haugh
Thomas Knapton, 37, Rawmarsh
John Knapton, 16 (son of above)
James Westerman, 16, Rawmarsh
William Hobson, 20, Thorpe
Thomas Whitehead, Rawmarsh
Richard Robinson, 18, Rawmarsh
Thomas Sylvester, Rawmarsh
Abraham Thompson, 27, Haugh
Joseph Firth, 11, Rose Hill

George Knapton, 51, Rawmarsh
Eli Bigg, 27, Rawmarsh
Joshua Roberts, 16, Rawmarsh
William Barrowclough, 19, Hooton Roberts (son of Charles, the banksman)
William Bownes, 18, Rawmarsh (an orphan)

Two who died later were William Bownes from Rawmarsh and, probably, Joseph Bownes, Rawmarsh (who, it was said, was 'not likely to recover').

(11) Pit: Elsecar Low Colliery

Location: Hemingfield, near Wombwell
Type: Explosion
Fatalities: 10
Date: Wednesday 22 December 1852

Coroner Thomas Badger was kept very busy during the middle years of the nineteenth century. New Elsecar Colliery exploded a year after the Warren Valley disaster, so local families experienced another very grim Christmas. The pit, consisting of two shafts, had been working for about five years and was regarded as being one of the safer pits since it was in the hands of the Earl Fitzwilliam and his very able engineer Benjamin Biram. The fiery Barnsley seam was worked at a depth of about 153 yards. Ventilation was provided by a large underground fan powered by a surface steam-engine. The air was diverted into two currents, towards the north and south workings. New developments included driving 'bordgates' towards two new pits which were being sunk to further improve the ventilation.

As at Warren Vale and other mines in the area fire-triers were employed to test for gas prior to the main body of workers descending the mine. At mid-day, on 22 December, the 'triers' had gone off duty. There were about 140 men and boys in the pit. For about half an hour, a boy hurrier propped open the trap-door which controlled the ventilation flow via the west bordgate. As a result there was a build-up of gas in the upper parts of the bordgates. The proper ventilation was restored after the door was closed. Unfortunately, the gas was carried in the current, reaching a place where a team of men were working, one of them with the top of his Davy lamp unscrewed (so he could work in better light) and an explosion occurred. Eight men were killed outright, two others dying from their injuries on the same day – and there were at least twelve other casualties, several of them with injuries likely to stop them working in a mine again.

News of the disaster was reported in the Christmas Eve edition of the *Sheffield and Rotherham Independent* under the heading FEARFUL COLLIERY EXPLOSION, NEAR ELSECAR:

> *One of those fearful calamities of which this neighbourhood has of late years been too frequent occurred on Wednesday afternoon, at the Elsecar Low Colliery belonging to Earl Fitzwilliam, situate at Hemingfield, a small hamlet about three miles from Wentworth Woodhouse, and nine from Sheffield.*

Those killed were:

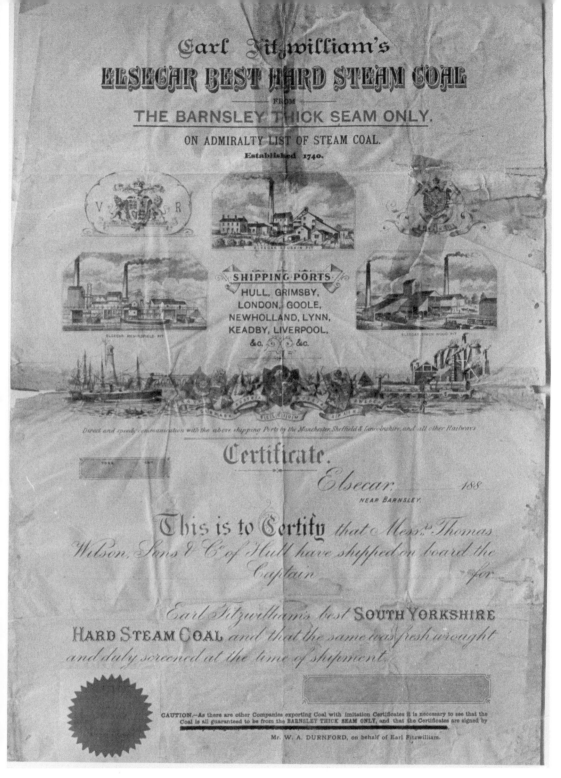

An 1880s advertisement extolling the virtues of 'Best Hard Steam Coal' from Earl Fitzwilliam's Elsecar colliery. AK Clayton/Brian Elliott

Benjamin Fletcher, aged 28, Stubbing, who left a widow and 3 children

Joseph Stenton, 22, Jump, unmarried (another report states he was married and left a widow and 3 children)

William Dickinson, Kit Royd, 33, widow and 4 children

Jonathan Walker, 47, Elsecar, widower, 7 children

George Mallinder, 28, Kit Royd, widow and 4 children (another report says 1 child)

John Mallinder, 17, unmarried (a relative of the above)

John Cooper, 16, Kit Royd (brother-in-law of the above)

Henry Addy, 17, Elsecar

Thomas Hirst, 42, widow and 4 children

Joseph Jowett, 14 (the last brought out, died the same evening)

The injured list included John Rigby (20, very burnt); Isaac Walker (hit and buried by a chair of coals); George Lindley (22, slightly injured); James Moulson (22, much injured, turned deranged); John Ballison (43, a newcomer, burnt); John Guest (burnt and bruised); Charles Sellers (14, much injured); Uriah Burgin (30, much injured); Thomas Hutchinson (30, burnt); Joseph Rawson (35, severely injured); Ralph Mares (35, slight); William Hemsworth (slightly burnt).

Charles Morton, Her Majesty's Inspector of Mines, questioned surviving miners at the inquest and found that though Davy lamps were in use they were often 'unscrewed' and blasting was carried out with gunpowder 'fired by touch-paper'. The fact the colliery had been accident-free for its five years of operation may have contributed to the general feeling that such practices were safe. John T Jeffcock, the colliery's eminent viewer admitted that the system of using lamps 'could be better', also stating that there were no printed rules, a situation which was quite common in the district. Benjamin Biram, the Earl's very able colliery adviser, agreed with the cause of the explosion and referred to his newly-invented safety lamp which gave off four times more light and was cheaper than others but could not 'urge its use under pits in his control'.

The usual 'accidental death' verdict was delivered by the inquest jury, with a strong recommendation that the suggestions made by the Inspector to improve the working of the mine should be carried out.

(12) Pit: Lundhill Colliery

Location: Hemingfield, near Wombwell
Type: Explosion
Fatalities: 6
Date: Tuesday 22 August 1854

On 22 March 1853 the first sod at the new Lundhill (also spelt Lund Hill) Colliery was formerly cut by the proprietors, William Taylor of Redbrook, Barnsley and Mr Greaves of Manchester, at Hemingfield. Each partner then placed £1 under the sod 'as an opening gift' to the workmen. With sinking well underway, an Easter supper was held for the workers, at the Three Horse Shoes Inn, Wombwell. Also present was the local landowner, Mr Swift, whose toast of 'Success to Lundhill Colliery' was greeted by a round of applause. The two pit sinkers, named as William Dickinson and George Whitehead, were each presented with a sovereign 'for the satisfaction they had given in

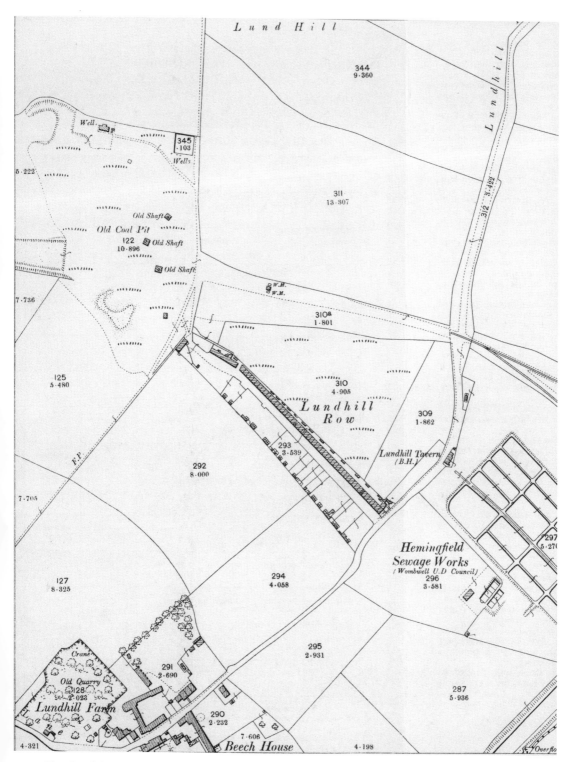

The site of the Lundhill colliery shafts and Lundhill Row can be seen on this large scale map published in 1905. Courtesy of the Ordnance Survey

the work'. Another notable presence at the supper was Mark Gomersall, the former agent for the Hopwood Colliery company, now employed at Lundhill.

In terms of human happiness, success never came to Lundhill Colliery. Even before the pit was fully operational, just thirteen months after the celebrations described above, a massive explosion occurred, resulting in the deaths of six men, causing considerable underground and surface damage. Fortunately the accident occurred in August, during the traditional Feast Week holiday, when many men were absent from work, otherwise the number of fatalities could have been larger. Although the pit's owners escaped reprimand, there were some very telling comments against their subsequent attitude and actions from Charles Morton, HM Inspector of Mines. It took a further eight months, until 14 April 1855, before the first coal was extracted. Then, within two years, on a cold February day in 1857, Lundhill fired again and became the scene of one of the worst tragedies in British mining history.

Sinking a new, deep mine always took many months of hard and skilful work by the men and the contractor, who had to overcome a variety of practical problems. Among the most feared hazards were water and gas. Lundhill had both in abundance.

There were two shafts, sited about 30–40 yards from each other. The drawing pit was about 75 yards deep, the other a little deeper. The sinkers and workmen were within a short distance of the coal bed, reached by a borehole which allowed water to drain away. Ominously, gas also came from this borehole on a frequent basis. For several days work was stopped because of the water problem, therefore resumption of work needed to take place with extreme caution in view of the build-up of gas. Incredibly, both the proprietors' mining agent, Mr Peace and the sinking contractor, Mr Jepson, were absent when work restarted and there was no prior underground inspection. It is hard to imagine such a situation today but, in the absence of any instructions, several men descended the pit carrying candles for light. Within five minutes there was a great explosion. The force of the blast was so fierce that one man was blown up and out of the shaft and another, the banksman at the pit-top, was blasted skywards and over a wall. Three others were killed instantly. Another died later. The heavy, wooden headgear was dislodged from the pit-bank and 'smashed to pieces', and debris thrown a distance of 50 yards.

A report in the *Leeds Intelligencer* of 26 August 1854 blamed the accident on an 'incautiously exposed' light, saying that the culprit was Noah Ely. The five men who died immediately were named as:

Noah Ely, aged 32, who left a widow and 4 or 5 children
James Batty, 23, banksman, single
William Hulse, 30
William Davies, 50, married
Matthew Pollard, 50

The overworked district coroner, Mr Badger, ordered the bodies to be 'locked up', not even allowing them to be washed until after the inquest, presumably to safeguard evidence. Unfortunately James Batty's remains had not been 'collected together' even by the Wednesday as he had been 'literally blown to pieces'. New legislation also required that Charles Morton, HM Inspector of Coal Mines, was called to attend the investigation.

Miners working by candlelight. The use of candles continued to be used in some so-called safe Yorkshire mines up to the late 1930s.
Author's collection

The inquest, held on the Thursday, at the Ship Inn, Wombwell resulted in the customary 'accidental deaths' verdict and the colliery owners acquitted of any culpability. There was mild criticism of the sinking contractor, John Jepson, who 'ought to have had men in whom he can place a little confidence, and [used] the means of ventilation which had been placed at his disposal'. It was also stated that had Noah Ely [or Heeley] acted with 'more caution the accident might not have occurred.' A second inquest was held a few days later on the body of the sixth victim. Once again, the proprietors were exonerated from any blame but Morton referred to the 'unwonted and extraordinary exertions' (via an experienced legal team and a barrage of expert witnesses) made by the colliery's management 'to shield themselves from an unfavourable verdict'. Damningly, some men who had survived the blast had been 'tampered with and were reluctant to answer any questions', presumably in fear of losing their jobs. The Inspector also stated that the village constable had selected the jury 'from the immediate vicinity of the colliery and from a class not likely to act independently or to give umbrage to the proprietors', concluding that 'it was not surprising that the second verdict was not unlike the first.'

All Saints', Darfield.
Photo: Brian Elliott

Tramming was back-breaking work. Again, note the position of the candle. Author's collection

Snap time, twenty minutes for a drink and a bite to eat. NUM

Typical short report from The Times *informing readers about the explosion at Warren Vale, Rawmarsh, 23 December 1851.* Author's collection

Getting coal using a pick was hot work even when standing in water. Author's collection

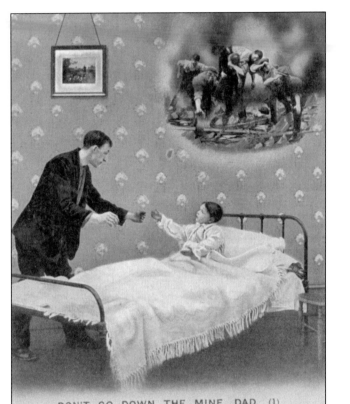

DON'T GO DOWN THE MINE, DAD. (1)

A miner was leaving his home for his work,
  When he heard his little child scream;
He went to his bedside, his little white face,
  "Oh, Daddy, I've had such a dream:
I dreamt that I saw the pit all afire,
  And men struggled hard for their lives;
The scene it then changed, and the top of the mine
  Was surrounded by sweethearts and wives."

WORDS BY PERMISSION OF THE LAWRENCE WRIGHT MUSIC CO.,
29, CONDUIT STREET, LEICESTER.
BAMFORTH (Copyright).

Part Three
Upon That Fatal Morn
Lundhill, 1857

'The mode of coal working in the Barnsley district was the most wretched and dangerous that I ever saw.'

Mr Coe, underground steward, Lundhill Colliery, 11 April 1857

'I hate a dirty wife and a dirty house, but I would sooner see both than any firedamp should abide and lodge in my pit.'

John Sutcliffe, manager, Gawber Hall Collieries, 1857

A young trammer at work in a Yorkshire pit. It was a back-hurting job in low roadways. 'Trammer's scab', following cuts and abrasions to the back bone was a common occupational complaint. Note the candle. Author's collection

(13) Pit: Lundhill Colliery

Location: Hemingfield, Wombwell
Type: Explosion
Fatalities: 189
Date: Thursday 19 February 1857

> *At five o'clock he left his home,*
> *Upon that fatal morn;*
> *And little thought upon the road*
> *He never must return.*
>
> *He reached the pit and did descend,*
> *To labour underground,*
> *While danger did each step attend,*
> *And darkness all around.*
>
> *We hope the Lord received his soul,*
> *With Him always to dwell;*
> *The sufferings he did undergo,*
> *No mortal tongue can tell.*

[From the memorial card in respect of George Dawson, aged 26, of West
Melton who was killed at Lundhill Colliery on 19 February 1857]

The churchyard at Darfield is situated in the most picturesque of settings, on a hill over-looking the Dearne. A wander around will benefit the visitor since there are some very interesting gravestones and memorials. The late John Betjeman, when he was Poet Laureate, came here specially to look at the grave of that great champion of the working-class, Ebenezer Elliott (1789–1849), the 'Corn Law Rhymer' or 'Poor Man's Poet' who lived nearby, at Hargate Hill. Betjeman may also have noticed, situated prominently at the far end of the old churchyard, a soot-black obelisk. The work of Oxley, the well-known family of stonemasons, the main inscription explains that the monument was erected to commemorate the 'LUNDHILL EXPLOSION' in which 189 men and boys lost their lives 'OF WHOSE BODIES, ONE HUNDRED AND FORTYSIX ARE BURIED NEAR THIS PLACE'. Four mass graves were used for the churchyard interments located in an unmarked area near the monument. The stonemason appears to have had difficulty in finding sufficient space for 'FORTY SIX', inscribing 'FORTYSIX' (with no space between the words) instead. In any case this number may be an error or placed there for convenience since a figure of 149 is given by the coroner. The figure 'NINE' would have required an extra space, therefore impossible to accommodate. Any error may also relate to the long process of raising sufficient funds to pay for a substantial memorial. On the second anniversary of the disaster, when a special service was held in Darfield church a collection was 'made towards the erection of a monument in Darfield church-yard . . . '. It may have taken a further year for the monument to be erected. Inscribed at the bottom of the plaque can be seen the Old Testament phrase: 'PREPARE TO MEET THY GOD.' Taken from Amos IV, v.12, this

All Saints' churchyard at Darfield contains a wealth of interesting memorials. One of the few still protected by its original iron railings is the grave of Ebenezer Elliott, the famous 'Corn Law Rhymer' and champion of the poor.
Photo: Brian Elliott

was a popular Victorian extract from the scriptures, chosen to highlight the great uncertainty of life, therefore particularly relevant to working people and more so for those that worked in coal mines. Sadly, some of the memorial has suffered from graffiti in recent years, the perpetrators probably older than the many boys killed in this great tragedy of 150 years ago. This monument, listed because of its architectural and historic value, is of national importance, a grim reminder of an industrial past which should never be forgotten.

By the 1850s mining disasters had become big news stories for Victorian newspapers and the new illustrated magazines. Lundhill was probably the first pit disaster to make the front page of the prestigious *Illustrated London News* (ILN) and detailed coverage appeared for several days in *The Times* and for many weeks in the regional press.

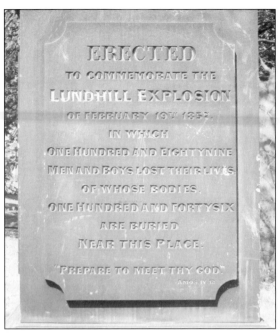

ERECTED
TO COMMEMORATE THE
LUNDHILL EXPLOSION
OF FEBRUARY 19TH 1857.
IN WHICH
ONE HUNDRED AND EIGHTYNINE
MEN AND BOYS LOST THEIR LIVES,
OF WHOSE BODIES,
ONE HUNDRED AND FORTYSIX
ARE BURIED
NEAR THIS PLACE.
"PREPARE TO MEET THY GOD"
AMOS IV 12

Left: *The now soot-black (and sadly vandalised)
obelisk to the victims of the Lundhill disaster,
prominent in Darfield churchyard. The open
ground in front of the memorial was used for mass
burial.* Photo: Brian Elliott
Above: *PREPARE TO MEET THY GOD: detail
of the main inscription, Lundhill disaster
memorial, Darfield churchyard.* Photo: Brian Elliott

Photography was in its infancy and it was several decades before actual photographic images could be reproduced. There was a reliance on drawings and prints to supplement the column-filled pages of small print. The new London magazines dispatched artists of Royal Academy standard to capture and reconstruct the scene of disasters, based on eyewitness reports and, if available, the work of pioneering local photographers. It appears that photographic images were used since they are acknowledged as such – though not named – on some of the artwork. If the photographer was local it may have been the work of Job Walker, a former miner who had established his business in Barnsley in about 1854, also offering a mobile service. Whatever the origin, it was the artists' dramatic sketches that made the magazines so popular with the Victorian public.

The voyeuristic part of human nature increasingly came to the fore at major disasters when, through the developing railway system, hundreds, sometimes many thousands of people travelled to colliery towns. Pit disasters had become great public spectacles. Contemporary reports frequently contrasted the suffering of the bereaved with the 'entertainment' element of the crowd:

Every train today has brought a large number of excursionists, who, by their conduct, seemed bound to a fair or country fête rather than visitors to the scene of a frightful calamity. At two o'clock there were from ten to fifteen thousand persons on the spot; and few indeed were those who appeared to think they were standing immediately over the bodies of nearly two-hundred men, hurried without a minute's notice into eternity. In the dense crowd before them the loud laugh and jest were heard incessantly. A few more serious ones sang hymns. [ILN, 28 February 1857]

Estimates of crowd size are often exaggerated in contemporary reports but even making an allowance for this, the number of spectators descending on what was then a relatively isolated and rural area is staggering, equivalent to a good attendance at many modern professional football grounds.

Despite relatively recent events highlighting the dangers of working at Lundhill, the colliery company had successfully recruited about 290 men and boys, about two-thirds of whom worked on the day shift, the remainder at night. Many lived in adjacent communities in and around Wombwell, Hemingfield and Jump, walking to the pit each day. A few miners came in from outlying areas such as Ardsley, Darfield, West Melton, Monk Bretton, Worsbrough Dale, even as far as Gawber (near Barnsley). However, a significant number of Lundhill employees resided in a new purpose-built settlement within the shadow of the colliery. Consisting of over fifty cottages and a chapel, Lundhill Row was also served by a public house, the *Lundhill Tavern*, now the only surviving building. The entire area was extensively landscaped for recreational purposes during the 1990s, including the provision of a golf course.

Lundhill Row, long demolished, was the distinctive small community originally established to serve Lundhill colliery. The headstocks in the distance are of the later Cortonwood colliery. Only the Lundhill Tavern (now The Tavern) remains. Author's collection

Rare photographs showing the Lundhill Wesleyan Church, Lundhill Row, shortly before demolition in the 1960s. Note the gas light. The headstocks served a local pumping shaft. AK Clayton/Brian Elliott

In 1857 Lundhill Colliery was one of the largest and deepest pits in Yorkshire. There were now three shafts. Number 1, the water pumping and downcast, was the shallowest, at 77 yards (and 10 ft diameter), sunk to the Abdy seam; number 2, used as a downcast and for coal-drawing, was 217 yards deep (11 ft 4 inch diameter); and number 3, the upcast or furnace shaft, was 214 yards deep (9ft 3 inch diameter). The deep downcast shaft provided access to the principal coal of the district – the famous Barnsley seam. Workings were extensive, extending several hundred yards from the pit bottom. Coal output was good – 500–600 tons per day and the pit worked for six days a week. No doubt the Taylor partnership, which now included Simpson, Stewart and Galland, were very pleased with what appears to have been a profitable concern.

On the morning of the disaster there were about 220 men and boys at work underground at Lundhill (perhaps a 'rounded' figure). According to local press reports, twenty-two of the day-workers who lived at Lundhill Row fortuitously ascended one of the shafts (probably No. 2) at mid-day so that they could have some dinner at home. The rest of the shift stayed put, consuming their 'snap' as usual, in workings away from the pit bottom. The men underground had barely finished their meal when, at about 12.30 (some reports say 12.20) there was, what the *Illustrated London News* described as 'a fearful explosion' (and the official report as 'an astounding and fearful explosion') so large that it 'shook the ground for a great distance around'. The blast was so violent that the cage that normally carried the corves or tubs of coal was blasted up the deep drawing shaft and into the wooden headgearing over the pit mouth, its rope and chain tangling

The 1857 Lundhill disaster attracted huge crowds of visitors during the several days following the explosion, captured here in the Illustrated London News. www.cmhrc.co.uk

This dramatic image of Lundhill colliery 'firing' was prominent in the Illustrated London News *of 1857.* www.cmhrc.co.uk

The damage at the top of the Lundhill shaft. www.cmhrc.co.uk

with the pulley wheels. When this happened after explosions there was always a delay before equipment could be re-used or an alternative system could be set up for a brave descent of the shaft, providing of course it was deemed 'safe' to do so. At the same time, from the top of the furnace shaft ' . . . a prodigious amount of dust, smoke, and flame arose to a considerable height, accompanied by a large report . . .' [official report]. The whole scene perhaps resembled a compact version of the kind of spectacular film footage we have seen in modern times at Flixborough chemical plant disaster and, very recently, at Buncefield Oil Terminal.

After reporting that the pit was on fire underground, therefore cutting off any attempt to reach the trapped men, the *Illustrated London News* referred to ' . . . flames ascending the air shaft . . .' , reaching skywards 'more than twenty yards above the top' and 'illuminating the country for a distance around'.

A group of men, including Joseph Coe, William Porter Maddison, Robert Charles Webster, John Warhurst, William Beevors and William Utley eventually managed to descend the drawing shaft, finding twenty 'scorched and injured' survivors. They were successfully extracted from the pit and the underground search continued. What a dangerous task it was, described as follows in Inspector Charles Morton's report:

> *The most dreadful havoc had been and still was going on around them; the dead bodies of men and horses lay among confused heaps of overturned corves, shattered doors, broken timber, and fallen roof stone; the furnace and its arches were in ruins; the solid coal in . . .*

Some men were killed in the roof falls following the explosion, others expired from the afterdamp.
www.cmhrc.co.uk

Horses and pit ponies were often killed in disasters. It was never easy to remove them from the workings. www.cmhrc.co.uk

Rescue workers shroud their dead colleagues and carry out human remains, scenes repeated in many South Yorkshire pits during the 1850–1880 period. ww.cmhrc.co.uk

ILLUSTRATED TIMES

(THE RIGHT OF TRANSLATION AND REPRODUCING ILLUSTRATIONS IS RESERVED.)

No. 97.—Vol. 4. LONDON, SATURDAY, FEBRUARY 28, 1857. PRICE 2½D.—STAMPED, 3½D.

THE BUDGET AND THE MINISTRY.

THE first blush of satisfaction produced by the news that the "war nine-pence" was abolished, was not very lasting. People read the debates, and considered our recent financial history, and fell into a state of doubt, soon succeeded by a state of disgust. First, of course, came the consideration of that growing expenditure to which we called attention last week. What is our position with regard to it? This is the important point, since all hopes of relief from direct or indirect taxation must rest on the possibility of our reducing the present increasing expenses of Government.

In the first place, let the reader dismiss the idea altogether, that, with the expenditure as it at present is, the income-tax will ever come off. The absurdity of *that* supposition rises prominent out of all these discussions. It has been proved, that, what with the war loans and the reductions announced, the revenue for 1858-9 must be below that for 1857-8 by five millions and a half. How, then, is the income-tax, in its old and (now that we are at peace) offensive form, to come off in 1860? It is out of the question. Besides, we are only supposing at present that things go on during the intervening years in an ordinary manner. An entirely new war may arise, under Lord Palmerston's auspices, in the interval. In that case, the income-tax will be up again, and the tea and sugar duties permanently "arrested" in their very gentle decline; for, as tea is said to be a slow poison,—so, relief from taxes on it seems to be a slow benefit.

Well. We shall be told that it is not Sir Cornewall Lewis's business to get the income-tax off by 1860,—that it is only his business to stave off the question three years more, and that meanwhile a reduction *is* achieved. But considerations like this will scarcely do for the country, which grows alarmed at the systematic increase above mentioned. The actual relief promised at present is not great. It leaves a heavy direct tax, and heavy indirect

THE LUND HILL COLLIERY EXPLOSION: RESCUING THE SURVIVORS.—(SEE PAGE 131.)

taxes (just lightened enough to show that we are not absolutely at war with a great Power); but it leaves an uneasiness which is as bad as the burdens themselves, by leaving it probable that three years hence will find us as embarrassed as ever. The deficiencies—to provide for which the income-tax was renewed in our own time—are, according to the policy of Palmerston's Government, to become again parts o our system.

The fact is, that when the Budget was first introduced, the rough outward fact of the reductions misled people they thought Government was acting with wonderful liberality. Mr. Gladstone—in that speech of last week, the ability of which will be long remembered—put the world right as to this. He reminded us that the war taxes on coffee, &c., lapsed by Act of Parliament, not by grace of Government; and he showed that, in money, the reductions boasted of did not amount to so much as was pretended. We shall not repeat figures already diffused over the kingdom, in illustration of this *exposé*; we shall confine ourselves to recalling the general result—viz., that Mr. Gladstone's analysis reduced the really voluntary and positive reductions of the Government, for 1857-8, from nearly twelve millions to something over three. Of course it is natural that journals, which (for reasons we never could understand) indissolubly connect the present Government with Liberalism, should pooh-pooh such criticism; but it is the criticism of a man whose experience is as great as his parts, and who inherits the really liberal financial views of our last great statesman. Mr. Gladstone's own Budget of 1853 produced a surplus (in spite of military expenditure) of three millions; and his object in rigidly investigating the pretensions of the present one, has been to recall the necessity of fulfilling the promises then virtually made to the people.

There are reasons for believing that Government showed this spending turn, under the idea that the public was itself in the old reckless war temper. The

MINERS' COTTAGES, LUND HILL COLLIERY: RELATIVES RUSHING TO THE SCENE OF THE EXPLOSION.—(SEE PAGE 131.)

the upcast shaft had ignited; burning masses of coal were tumbling down the sides, and the fire was raging fiercely and spreading rapidly; the stables were in flames, and combustible gas showed itself in the safety lamps within a short distance . . . Smoke and after-damp were very strong in some parts, and the firedamp prevailed in every boardgate.

When the search and rescue party returned to the surface, at seven-thirty in the evening, 'a column of flame 100 feet high rushed furiously from the furnace pit' and, with 'blazing embers and sparks' rising even higher, shedding 'a lurid glare on the sorrowful and despairing countenances of an immense assembly of men, women and children'. It was a timely escape for the explorers. The Sheffield Fire Brigade arrived but extinguishing the fire was hopeless. Local pit managers who had come to Lundhill to offer assistance met with the colliery managers and a decision was made to cap the two downcast shafts. When this was achieved, using planks and clay, the flames at the top subsided and stopped, though thick smoke continued to come from the furnace shaft which was left open.

On the morning after the disaster Charles Morton, the regional HM Inspector of Mines, had a meeting with two experienced mining engineers, J T Woodhouse of Derby, Henry Holt of Wakefield, and the Lundhill viewers. A plan was devised and approved by Nicholas Wood and George Elliott, two more eminent engineers who had been recruited from Durham to give advice. All four 'visiting' engineers were given the responsibility of directing the opening up of the mine and the recovery of the bodies, assisted by a local group of viewers. The mouth of the furnace pit was closed apart from an 8-inch aperture which allowed gas to escape. The use of water was the main tactic employed to extinguish the fires, a local stream being diverted into the workings for this purpose. Careful records were kept of the gradually decreasing temperature in all the shafts. It took a month for the mine to be flooded and then drained, great care being taken with regard to the use of safety lamps due to the ever-present danger of gas emission. Two ventilation fans, loaned by Earl Fitzwilliam, were fixed above the upcast shaft, powered by steam from the colliery boilers.

It was not until 17 April, almost two months after the explosion, that the very grim task of recovering the bodies began. The process was described in the report as 'nauseous, arduous, an[d an] hazardous undertaking'. In order to combat the stench 'neutralising and deodorizing compounds' were liberally used and the men were given practical advice concerning the handling of the corpses from Mr Holland, the local Inspector of Burial Grounds. Six teams of twelve men were deployed, each man working a maximum of four hours, and each team containing two deputies and at least one assistant engineer. Stephenson safety lamps were used. The men wore charcoal respirators, covering the mouth, and gloves. The dead colliers and horses found at the pit bottom were removed first. By 22 May over a hundred corpses had been recovered and 'nearly the whole of the remainder' had been dug out from roof falls and debris before the end of July. A few bodies may have been left undiscovered in the mine, 'named' by elimination. Early press reports describe the planned arrangements for the identification of bodies:

Opposite: *Front page of the* Illustrated Times *following the Lundhill disaster of 1857. Such was the scale of the tragedy that Lundhill was probably the first disaster to appear on the front page of London-based magazines which had national and international readerships.* Author's collection

Another scene from the Illustrated Times *showing the recovery of bodies at Lundhill.* Author's collection

It is intended to erect a shed capacious enough to contain the whole number, and as the bodies are brought up, they will be placed in coffins, which are in the course of preparation, and deposited in this structure. To each of them will be attached a ticket, containing (if the deceased be identified) his name, otherwise a number according to the order in which it is brought up. Every effort has been made by the proprietors to ascertain the names of all in the pit [ILN, 28 February 1857].

The above report concluded that 182 'had perished' but that 'even this number will probably be increased upon subsequent inquiry'. This statement was based on local information rather than actual bodies recovered.

The last body reported to be got out, on 16 July 1857, was that of Matthew Broadhead.

A graphic part of the official report summarises the extent of damage to both the mine and the miners:

Bulky balks of timber were broken; substantial brick arches and stoppings were prostated; thick pack walls and firmly fixed chocks were knocked down; strong malleable iron rails were riven up and contorted; stout wooden door frames were split and iron door bands bent; doors, brattices, and corves were shivered to fragments; two human bodies were dismembered, and the pieces scattered over a space of forty yards; the heads or limbs of other corpses were blown from the trunks; many were so dreadfully burnt and mutilated as to be unrecognisable; one man was found transfixed with the pick with which he had been in the act of cutting coal; a second appeared to have been killed (as if by instantaneous shock) while drilling a hole; and several were sitting at dinner . . . some of the unfortunate victims were neither burnt nor bruised, but seem to have expired quietly under the insidious and suffocating influence of after-damp.

The inspector and engineers toured the underground workings in order to try to locate the seat of the explosion. The 'greatest violence' was evident between No. 4 and No. 5 boardgates but the blast of air originated from the No. 1 or furnace broadgate. It was concluded that the explosion began on the northern or north-western side of the mine and that firedamp had accummulated after a roof fall, 'but it was impossible to determine exactly in what place and by what means the gas was first ignited'. However, candles, 'with their tallow melted off' were found in the back boardgate and several slits.

Coroner Badger presided over many mine accident and disaster inquests but such was the magnitude of Lundhill that – at least regionally – the proceedings were unprecedented in their scale and extent. Over eleven different days the jury heard testimony from sixty witnesses over a three-month period. This included evidence provided by several men who survived the explosion:

William Corbridge (a deputy who had been employed at Lundhill for three years) said:

When the explosion happened, I and five others were getting dinner, near to the pit drawing bottom. I descended the pit on Thursday morning, about four o'clock; went with a Davy-lamp, and examined the broadgates and banks on the south side, and found the places safe. I also examined the goafs [waste areas] and found no gas in them.

Corbridge confirmed that all was safe in both the north and south side of the mine. He also said that though Davy-lamps were used 'where necessary', candles with 'naked lights' were also in general use. The furnace was 'well-attended to' but the packwall builders who 'ought regularly to have used safety lamps' appeared to have been in the habit of unscrewing the gauzes, but he admitted that he did not lock them according to Special Rule 1.

Abraham Levitt, a packer, who was sitting in a cabin at the pit bottom when the explosion occurred, said that he 'worked with a candle, but at times used a safety lamp'. Levitt was of the opinion that the oil 'was so bad we could not make the lamps burn', confirming that the gauzes were 'rarely locked' and 'sometimes we screwed them off'. He admitted that the packers were disobeying rules and thought that the explosion was 'caused by a fall of roof'.

Most of the miners questioned who had come out of the pit early in the morning of 19 February after completing their night shift spoke about the widespread use of candles. John Robinson even spoke about there being 'too much air which wasted the candles' and considered the pit 'as safe as I had seen it' during his night shift.

Edward Simmon, was one of the fortunate survivors, despite working well away from the pit bottom. He recalled his experiences as follows:

I was working in a boardgate on the dip side of the pit, about 140 yards from the pit bottom. In running to the shaft, I met the afterdamp, and it nearly choked me; but I laid down until the fresh air came again, and I was afterwards rescued.

William Hubbershaw was working even further away, some 200 yards from the drawing shaft when the explosion occurred:

> Three persons were with me; one ran away, and he perished; but the other two came out with me. We remained in our place for several hours, and the air was so hot I thought we could not survive: we laid still, and then taking hold of one another, we made the best way to the pit bottom, where we found several persons alive, having passed over two or three dead bodies: my senses left me, and I do not remember who brought me up the shaft.

He went on to make the point that the packers, despite any deputy's comments, use naked lights near the goafs.

Candid and detailed evidence was given by Joseph Coe who was the principal viewer at Lundhill at the time of the explosion. He stated that he was in the pit the day before the explosion, though did not examine the south workings. The air currents were functioning normally and there were no indications of gas. He considered the packers who worked with naked lights were 'competent workmen'. 'Candles', he said, 'were used in this pit; and if any gas came out (by falls or otherwise) of the goaf, it was liable to ignite at the naked lights; and in my opinion, this has been the proximate cause of the explosion.' After explaining to the jury how the pit was ventilated he had more to say concerning the use of naked lights:

> Prior to the explosion, I considered it quite safe to work the Lundhill colliery with naked lights; but I should now recommend that every mine in the Barnsley district should be worked exclusively with safety lamps. As regards the system of working coal generally in this neighbourhood, I will venture to say (from my own experience in the North of England, in Staffordshire, and in Yorkshire) that the Barnsley mode of getting coal is the most wretched and the most dangerous that I know.

Coe appears to have been demoted to under-viewer at Lundhill by the time of the inquest, replaced by Henry Holt of Wakefield.

An expert witness, Nicholas Wood, an eminent mining engineer from Durham made a special contribution, including the following:

> This is the third great explosion in the Barnsley district that I have been called to investigate; and all the three have been caused by the use of naked lights under similar circumstances, and would have been avoided if safety lamps had been employed. I stated on the two former occasions that it was highly imprudent and hazardous to use naked lights in the vicinity of goaves; and I have repeated the statement very strongly before committees of both Houses of Parliament. I hope these terrible examples will induce a safer mode of working the coal and lighting the mines in this neighbourhood.

Wood's hopes and recommendations, as we shall see, were not universally acted on by both officials, pit managers and owners.

After the coroner at the inquest had 'lucidly summed up and ably commented on the evidence of numerous witnesses' the following verdict was given by the jury:

> That the deceased were killed by an explosion of carburetted hydrogen gas in Lundhill colliery, on the 19th February 1857; but there is no conclusive or sufficient evidence to show the immediate cause of the explosion. Therefore, the jury cannot come to the decision that it was criminally neglect, but accidental. They, however, must condemn the laxity of

discipline, and the non-observance of the special rules. The jury do not attach blame to the proprietors of the colliery, who were not cognizant of the loose discipline and misconduct of the under-viewer, deputies, and workmen.

Furthermore, the jury reiterated the importance of working with safety lamps as well as other safety improvements suggested by the engineers; and the 'heroic conduct' of those men who recovered the bodies. Finally, 'deep sympathy' was expressed to all the bereaved in this 'most disastrous accident'.

The Lundhill Coal Company immediately changed the management of the mine, placing it in the experienced hands of the noted Barnsley viewer John Brown, previously employed at the troubled Oaks Colliery.

At the time Lundhill was the worst disaster by far in British coal mining history, leaving 90 widows and 220 orphaned children. Just over half of the women had remarried by March 1860. The Lundhill Relief Fund realised £10,676, the Lundhill Coal Company (who lost an estimated £20,000 in the disaster) donating £500.

The lessons of Lundhill are plain to see in the recorded inquest evidence and the comments in Morton's official report. If there was one positive factor that this disaster conveyed to colliery owners and engineers, it was to bring attention to the great importance of good and adequate ventilation. William Hopton of Carlton, near Barnsley published a paper entitled *Conversation on Mines* which stimulated many weeks of discussion in the mining press. Central to Hopton's thesis was an examination of

The anonymous capped shafts of old Lundhill colliery can still be seen on the local golf course at Lundhill. Few players probably appreciate that this was the scene of a disaster of national proportions.
Photo: Brian Elliott

Lundhill's 'bad' ventilation which was the main motive for his publication. Nicholas Wood, one of the most eminent experts called to Lundhill, and President of the Institute of Mining was so impressed that he offered to pay for Hopton to become a member of the institute. Hopton declined because of the requirement to attend meetings at Newcastle which he could not afford to do. For his comments on Lundhill he was victimised and became something of an outcast, his family 'reduced to poverty'. Eventually Hopton moved to Lancashire where he was awarded a prize of £275 for a paper on *The Prevention of Catastrophes in Mines*.

New legislation and a larger and more effective inspectorate were clearly needed as a matter of great urgency. Meanwhile disasters continued with terrible consequences for the mining communities of South Yorkshire. Within ten years Lundhill was to lose its unenviable tag as the location of Britain's worst disaster, to a near neighbour and one that its viewer, John Brown knew very well.

Even after catastrophic disasters it was rare for pits not to function in some form or other. Lundhill not only reopened but became something of a show pit for London visitors. It operated until the late 1880s when its then owners, the Wombwell Main Coal Company, began winding Lundhill coal from Wombwell Main. Lundhill's last manager, William Gray, became manager at Wombwell Main. Any historic link with Lundhill ended in 1969 when Wombwell Main closed.

The fatality listing shown below may include some variation in spelling of surnames

Local professional photographer and former pitman Joe Short was responsible for this image of Mr and Mrs Rhodes of Lundhill Row, taken in the mid-1920s. No doubt they had stories to tell about the 1857 disaster. Joe Short/Wharncliffe Books

and ages. Some families were very badly affected by the disaster, losing the main bread-winner and one or more children, most notably the Kellets who suffered seven deaths. Mining was certainly a young man's occupation at this time, only five of the deceased listed as aged fifty or more. At least four boys were aged ten, just above the legal limit of working underground, but one wonders if any of them were younger; and six others were just eleven years old. The minimum age for working underground was raised to fourteen in 1911.

Lundhill

Dennis Bush (22)
Thomas Faulks (29)
John Cutt jnr (17)
George Cutt (16)
William Illingworth (32)
Thomas Hilton (24)
Joseph Simmonds (26)
Richard Wilkinson (35)
James Wilkinson (22)
Charles Barrowclough (22)
James Smith (23)
John Smith (39)
Robert Howarth (25)
Joseph Goodhall (24)
George Scholer (32)
Barney Bailey (40)
Edward Walker (27)
William Hutchinson (20)
Peter McAllister (26)
Samuel Abbott (10)
Thomas Kellett (17)
Samuel Hunt (32)
Edward Garbutt (36)
John Garbutt (11)
Elijah Beevors (18)
Joseph Backwood (23)
Alfred Windle (30)
William Monks (32)
Israel Hobson (20)
Samuel Schofield (25)
Richard Corbridge (27)
Matthew Cowen (15)
John Harper (20)
A Nicholson (17)

Joseph Allenson (23)
John Cutt snr (40)
William Cutt (16)
Ezra Illingworth (10)
John Illingworth (10)
Joseph Crossland (32)
Edward Simmonds (11)
Thomas Wilkinson (33)
Henry Barrowclough (26)
Joseph Smith (53)
John Smith (19)
James Smith (22)
Benjamin Batty (22)
George F Shepherd
John Malkin (22)
George Bailey (14)
James Walker (22)
Charles Ludrick (20)
Joseph Abbott (40)
Richard Kellett snr (33)
Richard Kellett jnr (13)
James Hunt (27)
Witham Garbutt (17)
Benjamin Beevors (23)
Elijah Crompton (19)
Robert Fletcher (55)
John Halliday (20)
John Hobson (?)
Levi Jackson (44)
Matthew Broadhead (25)
James Burthard (21)
Thomas Uttley (20)
Thomas Horne (24)
A N other (not named)

Wombwell

John Carr (14)
Stephen Depledge (13)

James Oldham (24)
James Ives (22)

William Smith (27)

William Greenwood (24)

Abraham Nettleton (22)

Henry Hawcroft (22)

Joseph Margison (38)

Joseph Harrison (38)

Joseph Harrison (18)

John Beevors (20)

John Grimshaw (32)

Joseph Grimshaw (42)

John Thompson (30)

H Mellor (22)

Samuel Parkinson (21)

Luke Hartley (20)

George Moore (50)

Robert Moore (43)

James Coates (34)

Charles Coates (29)

Edward Pollard (50)

James Pollard (49)

Robert Pullan (20)

Charles Kellett (28)

Joseph Kellett (19)

Charles Walker (24)

West Melton

Thomas Nortcliffe (17)

George Nortcliffe (15)

William Thompson (19)

Benjamin Guest (17)

John Frost (32)

George Dawson (26)

Amos James (30)

John Cooper (11)

George Townsend (19)

Robert Burland (20)

George Tattersall (29)

James Tattersall (19)

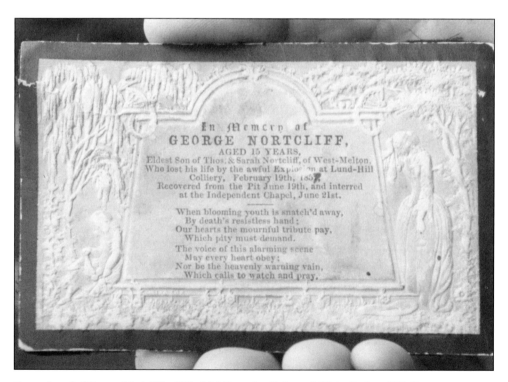

Funeral card of George Nortcliffe of West Melton who died, aged 15, in the Lundhill disaster. Cannon Hall Museum, Barnsley MBC/Photo: Brian Elliott

George Law (39)
Thomas Drury (32)
Thomas Logan (37)
William Mangham (25)
George Tunnacliffe snr (?)
William Webb (22)

Sampson Law (21)
James Drury (10)
Thomas Gray (22)
Charles Milner (22)
George Tunnacliffe (20)
Daniel Chisholm (27)

Hemingfield
John Denton (39)
John Russell (27)
George Gill (49)
John Scott (25)
Thomas Turner (17)
David Howarth (39)
Henry Booker (22)
William Horsfield (32)
E Knowles (30)
George Gee (25)
Arthur Dawson (13)
Edward Trainer (23)
Samuel Roebuck (24)

Thomas Denton (18)
Stuart Russell (17)
Stephen Turner (31)
John Hodgson (31)
Josiah Whitney (24)
John Ward (24)
John Booker (16)
William Moore (23)
Thomas Gee (27)
John Dawson (10)
Thomas Taylor or Levett (22)
Michael Baine (22)

Jump
George Thompson (37)
William White (25)
Richard Smith (25)
James Litchfield (26)
William Litchfield (11)
Thomas Farmer (26)

Henry Wilson (18)
Abraham Wildsmith (18)
George Mason (33)
Thomas Litchfield (22)
Richard Dunstan (33)
William Candlett (18)

Broomhill
Thomas Kitchen (38)
John Haley (22)
Samuel Thorp (16)
Thomas Kellett (39)
Joseph Blackburn (11)

Philip Dart (30)
Andrew Musgrave (33)
George Farmer (24)
William Kellett (10)

Old Factory (Wath)
Abraham Turner (21)
William Pickles (29)
John Wilkinson (22)
George Offenden (25)

George Foster (16)
George Mangham (24)
George Dyson (19)
N. McLaughlin (23)

Ardsley
John Stevenson (25)
Joseph Childs (23)
James Barrow (29)

William Dyson (17)
William Childs (19)
George Moss (17)

Worsbrough Dale

John Rooke (26) Benjamin Johnson (31)

William Thomas (?)

Newhill

George Law (29) John Philips (19)

Gawber

Joseph Lumb (33) John Lumb (11)

Darfield

Richard Marsden (24)

Monk Bretton

William Mitchell (61)

Part Four

Dickens and Crowds of Grimy Excursionists 1858–65

' . . . the train itself was under way and this time for what is called the black Yorkshire town of Barnsley . . . The town itself was white enough for all practical purposes, it was the visitors themselves who needed washing. The crowd of grimy excursionists oozed into the yard and satisfied themselves with tubs, butts and horse troughs.'

An engraving showing Edmunds Main, strategically located near to the Dearne and Dove Canal.
Author's collection

(14) Pit: Higham Colliery

Location: Higham Bottom, Higham, near Barnsley
Type: Explosion
Fatalities: 13
Date: Wednesday 15 February 1860

The late 1850s were a very unstable period on the South Yorkshire Coalfield. By October a strike affecting many collieries was declared over, after twenty-seven weeks; but a similar dispute began in West Yorkshire. Locally, there were often differences over price lists (set rates of pay), some coal companies resorting to 'lock-out' men who refused their terms. At Elsecar strikers were allowed to return to work only if they accepted old pay-rates and had no union affiliations. An unusual situation arose at Rawmarsh in the autumn of 1858 when there was a large meeting of striking miners from Warren Vale, Parkgate, Elsecar and other nearby pits. The Charlesworths had tried 'importing' thirteen 'blackleg' miners from West Bromwich to work at Warren Vale. The incomers were soon made fully aware of their situation by the strikers and returned home. At Edmonds Main, in January 1860, all 260 men 'gave in their tools, refusing to work again until the masters comply with their wishes'. The men's meagre home-coal allowance had been stopped.

The coal companies grumbled about the low price that they were getting for coal; but the burgeoning railway system, and the end of the monopoly enjoyed by the Great Northern line meant far better access to the London market. The Lundhill Coal Company, despite the great disaster of 1857, was still able to get over 3,000 tons of Barnsley coal to the capital during the first half of 1859.

If disputes were commonplace then so were everyday accidents. In the local press injuries and fatalities were reported in the local news columns most weeks. Here is a typical and rather sad account taken from the *Barnsley Record* of 31 March 1860:

> *Another feared colliery accident happened on Wednesday last, at the Edmonds Main Colliery [Worsbrough], to a young boy named Thomas Radcliffe, aged fourteen years . . . engaged as an horse-driver . . . the full ones [tubs] knocked him over and ran over one of his arms, nearly severing it from his body . . .*

Described as 'an orphan from Lancashire', Thomas Radcliffe had only worked at the pit for three weeks. After amputation, he was 'in a precarious state'.

In July 1859 over 200 London coal merchants and their friends came to the Barnsley area on an organised excursion to visit some of their suppliers. They were given a VIP tour. Two-thirds of the party, 'including some ladies' descended 'the celebrated Lundhill Colliery' before moving on to explore Edmonds Main where they expressed 'in phraseology scarcely understood by the workmen, their astonishment at the wonders they saw'. Many of the so-called 'interrogated miners' gave up responding due to the 'foreign language' of the visitors. The final stop was at the ill-fated Oaks, after which the train whisked them off to Barnsley for a grand dinner at the Corn Exchange. The most famous literary figure of the age, Charles Dickens, is mentioned as being a part of this touring party in an article by Joe Upton (from information provided by Barnsley Library) on the centenary of the Lundhill disaster, published in the *South Yorkshire Times* (26.1.1957), though the great man is not

mentioned in the contemporary news report. However, the *Barnsley Times* does record the presence of Dickens in Barnsley in its edition of 19 March 1859, a few months before the merchants' visit.

The government's Inspector of Mines, Charles Morton, was summoned to Charlesworths' Higham Colliery, about three miles from Barnsley, in 1857 when gas from the goaves ignited at the ventilation furnace. Cooper, the furnaceman, was the only person underground at the time, and managed to escape injury but ten pit horses were killed. John Ainsworth, the colliery's under-viewer, was advised that candles should not be used in the workings, only locked safety lamps. Subsequent inspections carried out in October of the same year and in December 1858 reiterated the recommendation. The official advice was ignored. Young pony-drivers continued to be allowed to use candles, with predictably disastrous consequences.

Whenever news occurred of a pit disaster, even when there was no obvious sight or sound, there was always a rush of people to the mouth of the colliery. Early in the afternoon of a mid-February day in 1860, little over a year since Morton's last inspection, John Ainsworth's period of underground duty was interrupted by what he later described as 'a slight noise'. Almost immediately a group of men came and told him that an explosion had occurred in the north area of the mine. Ainsworth ascended the shaft in order to obtain assistance. At the top, the banksman told him that he had not heard anything out of the ordinary, certainly no sound of an explosion. An exploratory party descended the shaft, proceeding in the direction of the area where fourteen men and boys were known to be working. Only four men were found alive, one of whom 'expired in the act of removal'. The *Barnsley Record* (published three days later) stated that the bodies 'presented a most painful appearance . . . They not only suffered from firedamp but also from . . . afterdamp . . . [and were] both bruised and burnt.' Several of the wives of the deceased miners were present when they were brought out of the pit, 'amid scenes of sorrow and wretchedness, the wringing of hands and the agony which could not be comforted . . . as each dead body, bruised and blackened, was recognised'. Details of those immediately killed (there are variations in the reported ages and spelling of names) included a grandfather and grandson:

Victorian artists did a marvellous job in capturing the drama of pit disasters, as can be seen in this example, published in the Illustrated London News. www.cmhrc.co.uk

Another typical Victorian illustration, showing the drama even more than a photograph would do.
www.cmhrc.co.uk

David Jagger, aged 72 [78?], coal-getter, Cawthorne (left a wife)
David Jagger (his grandson), 14, hurrier, Cawthorne
Levi Cawthorne [or John], 33 [35?], coal-getter, Cawthorne (left a wife and 3 children)
George Somers [or Summers] (stepson of Levi), 12, hurrier
Henry Blackburn, 12, horse-driver, Cawthorne
John Wilson, 40, coal-getter (left a wife and 4 children)
Joseph Wilson (son of John), 11 [14?], horse-driver
George [Joseph?] Clarke, 23, collier, Higham
John Whitehead, 27 [30?], Dodworth (left a wife and 4 children)
Henry Brown, 13 [12?], hurrier (son of Matthew, the colliery banksman)
William Depledge, 26, labourer, Gawber [from Barugh in one report]

The injured were named as Henry Wilson of Higham and his son, John, aged eleven; and 19-year-old Joseph Crossley.

Higham was a deep colliery (sometimes referred to as 'Higham Deep' and 'Old Silkstone') with extensive underground workings. There appear to have been three shafts, one of them measuring 220 or more yards in depth. At least 120 men and boys were said to have been normally working, so it was very fortunate that the fatalities were confined to one underground location.

The inquest opened at the Farmer's Arms public house, Higham, before the local coroner, T Taylor on the Thursday (16 February), the jury having been provided with a wagon for them to visit and view the bodies of the deceased in their respective homes. The identification process took two-and-a-half hours, and was followed the morning afterwards by an underground inspection of the colliery by the mines' inspector, Charles Morton, accompanied by John Ainsworth and the well-known local mining engineer, Richard Thorp.

The inquest met again on the Saturday evening, since one of the survivors, John Crossley, had died; and was then adjourned until Thursday 23 February. In the meantime there were the usual dreadful scenes of mourning:

The funerals [at Cawthorne] were attended by a large number of mourners, and the members of several sick clubs of which the deceased were members. The church was crowded, and the funeral service was impressively performed by the Rev. Charles Spencer Stanhope, assisted by the Rev. H. Badnall, during which there was scarcely a dry eye, many of the female congregation breaking into sobs. At the graveside some of the wives, mothers, brothers etc., seemed to give vent to the most poignant grief; and while the burial service was being performed over the dead, the widow of Levi Cawthorne swooned away, and had to be removed to a neighbouring house, where she had a succession of fits . . . [Barnsley Record, 22.2.1860]

David Jagger, although aged 72, was said to have recently 'espoused a young wife' and had talked about retiring from pit-work, preferring 'not to be burnt to death'. William Depledge was buried at Darton, and Joseph Crossley at Gawber.

The official inquest verdict was given as follows:

We are of the opinion that the explosion was purely accidental, at the same time earnestly recommend the Messrs Charlesworth to make general use of the Davy lamp.

Inspector Morton was, rightly, scathing both in his report and at the inquest, concerning the practice of using candles in Higham pit, especially after his previous

The gravestone of David Jagger, a victim of the Higham disaster, can still be seen in Cawthorne churchyard. Photo: Brian Elliott

recommendations, and was of the opinion that the origin of the explosion was 'at Joseph Wilson's candles' [in the Silkstone seam].

The inquest met yet again, with a new jury and at a different venue – the Miners' Arms – on the Monday evening, in respect of Henry Wilson, who had now died from his injuries and therefore was the thirteenth (and probably the last) victim of the disaster. John Giggle informed the jury that Wilson described to him that he was filling a corf when the explosion occurred, and threw himself to the ground, becoming unconscious. The usual 'accidental death' verdict was issued. The unfortunate Wilsons had lost three family members, with a fourth 'in a state not likely to recover'.

Explosions were becoming more frequent, especially in the Barnsley area. A few weeks after the Higham disaster, 8 March 1860, two stewards were killed at Strafford Main, near Barnsley, when they were removing brattices. In June 1861 twenty-three men received burns in an explosion at Old Mill Colliery (Barnsley) and one man was fatally affected by the afterdamp. A month later, two lives were lost in an explosion at East Gawber Hall Colliery (Darton, Barnsley). On 4 April 1862, at an hitherto safe pit at Chapeltown (near Sheffield) six men were killed in an explosion attributed to working with candles; and at the end of the year, at Edmunds Main, one of the large 'show pits' visited by the touring coal merchants from London, another major disaster occurred.

(15) Pit: Edmunds Main

Location: Worsbrough Dale, near Barnsley
Type: Explosion
Fatalities: 59
Date: Monday 8 December 1862

Edmunds Main was a new colliery, established in the Dove valley in 1855 by the John Tyas, Charles Bartholomew and Joseph Mitchell partnership (and functioning later as the Edmunds and Swaithe Main Company). The Barnsley coal was of excellent quality and the colliery was regarded as one of the safest and best ventilated in the area.

The disaster here was somewhat unusual in its circumstances compared with previous catastrophes in South Yorkshire pits. It originated when coal was ignited during heading or tunnelling work, carried out so as to create an underground link with Edmonds' new sister pit, Swaithe Main. This connection was by means of two parallel sloping passages or 'dip bordgates'. Despite the obvious dangers of working in the notoriously fiery Barnsley seam (firedamp had been ignited here only a week earlier), the four men employed in this work were using gunpowder – as well as candles for some of the light – blasting their way through the rock strata. They were encouraged in their task to proceed 'as quickly as possible' by George Lawton, the underground viewer (or manager) and offered a better rate of pay 'for wedging' (six shillings a yard as against five shillings a yard for blasting – plus a bonus of a sovereign [twenty shillings] to share if they could achieve fifty yards in two weeks). The men declined the 'incentive' which would have meant far harder work, really worth nine or ten shillings a yard, so continued with the relatively easier option: blasting with gunpowder – with disastrous consequences.

The coal fired between nine or ten in the morning and could not be extinguished. There were well over 200 men down the pit at the time, in Barnsley seam workings which extended a mile (W-E) by half-a-mile (N-S) from the pit bottom, over a hundred yards deep. George Lawton had to be brought from Swaithe, about a mile away. An attempt to make a stopping failed and flames issued through the two bordgates and towards the main underground workings. At eleven-thirty (am) a huge explosion occurred and many men flocked to the pit bottom, requiring assistance to get out. There

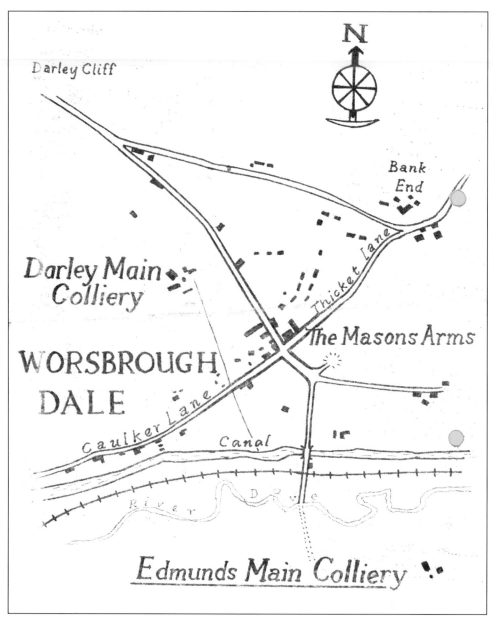

Sketch-map showing the sites of Darley Main and Edmunds Main collieries, Worsbrough Dale.
Author's collection

was great panic and confusion. The second explosion had destroyed communication with the pit-top. Many men and boys managed to ascend in a disciplined fashion, but there were at least fifty still stranded underground. George Lawton, along with his eldest son, Henry, along with Charles Frobisher, John Parkin and Benjamin Hoyland (the rescue party) were killed in a third explosion, at about one in the afternoon. Incredibly, more volunteers descended into the highly dangerous pit but, despite their efforts and bravery, the fires and afterdamp meant that, by four in the afternoon, they had to abandon their search.

Charles Morton, the erstwhile regional mines' inspector, after evaluating the situation, would not allow any further attempt to recover the bodies and advised the owners to flood the mine. Understandably, this did not go down very well with the waiting relatives and friends. Two independent mining engineers, J. T. Woodhouse of Derby and John Brown of Barnsley were consulted. A fourth explosion 'heard throughout Worsbrough Dale' confirmed the highly dangerous condition of the pit. There were three shafts at the colliery. The two downcasts were closed and the upcast filled with soil ten yards above the furnace drifts and water was run into the dip workings. This work was completed by the middle of the month of December 1862.

The inquest was held before the local coroner Thomas Taylor who, as we have seen, was no stranger to such occasions. The jury received evidence from thirty witnesses over

This image from the Illustrated London News *is of the trench that was cut from the canal so as to flood the Edmunds Main workings and put out the raging underground fires.* www.cmhrc.co.uk

A massive second explosion is shown in this drawing, taken from the Illustrated London News. *Fire blasts from the top of the Edmunds Main cupola shaft.* www.cmhrc.co.uk

four days. Key points of inquiry related to the measures that were (or were not) taken to warn the men following the initial fire and the ways and means used to try to extinguish the flames; and the condition of the pit immediately prior to the disaster. The primary cause of the disaster was the ignition of gas which emanated from the blasting operations when driving a heading towards the new shaft of Swaithe Main. It was found that although safety lamps were in use, hurriers used candles for their work, even though they came within a few yards of gaseous workings. George Pickering, the shot-firer who was working with the heading men, described how, after the blast when the coal was on fire, they tried to put the flames out with their jackets and by throwing wet slack; and later, with the help of George Lawton, to build a brick stopping. One of the men who managed to escape, William Davy, stated that more men would have been saved if they had been warned of the developing crisis.

The jury criticised the management of the colliery for allowing 'the dangerous use of gunpowder in blasting coal in the dip broadgates'. Representing the widows and orphans, Mr Sleigh, said that the verdict should be that of manslaughter but this was not accepted by the coroner and jury. One of the sixteen-man jury refused to endorse the standard 'open verdict' of 'accidental death'. A prosecution by the miners' union was dropped when the owners offered £1,500 in compensation.

SNATCHED FROM HIS HOME . . . The gravestone of John Parkin, aged 28, killed in the Edmunds Main disaster. Photo: Brian Elliott

Another remarkable feature of the Edmunds Main disaster, developing from recent similar events elsewhere, was the massive extent of public interest. The local press described how thousands of people – from all over the country – had arrived at the pit on the Sunday following the disaster. Fourteen thousand people passed through Barnsley Toll Bar from the direction of Sheffield and the south. A vast crowd assembled at and around the pit mouth, including an artist from the *Illustrated London News* who had to dash out of the way when the dramatic second explosion occurred.

Although no public memorial was commissioned for the victims of the disaster a special supplement appeared in the 20 December 1862 edition of the *Barnsley Chronicle*, listing 'the unfortunate sufferers'. Most of the deceased lived close by the pit, in Worsbrough Dale, or at nearby Worsbrough Common. The ages and number of dependants of some of those named in the supplement do vary slightly from the list shown here which may be more accurate:

George Firth (aged 31), Worsbrough Dale, married, 2 children
James Ewins (40), Barnsley, married, 2 children
Richard Hunt (19), Worsbrough Common, single
Charles Wildsmith (42), Worsbrough Common, married, 8 children
Matthew Bates (36), Worsbrough Dale, married, 3 children
Thomas Goldthorpe (38), Worsbrough Dale, married, 5 children
William Rigby (29), Barnsley, single
George Columbine (14), Worsbrough Common, boy
Thomas Wroe (otherwise Mitchell, 21), Worsbrough Common, single
Thomas Hammerton (alias Oxterbury, 40), Barnsley, married, 4 children
George Galloway (18), Worsbrough Common, single
Henry Palfreyman (50), Barnsley, married, 6 children
George Ogden (17), Worsbrough Common, single
William Sharrock (39), Worsbrough Common, married, 2 children
John Shaw (28), Barnsley, single
William Ogley (28), Worsbrough Common, married, 2 children
George Ogley (20)
James Ratcliffe (28), Worsbrough Dale, married, 1 child
James Tong (26), hurrier for Ratcliffe, married, 2 children
George Lawton (59), bottom steward, Worsbrough Dale, married, 1 child
Henry Lawton (27), son of George, deputy steward, single
William Parkinson (29), Worsbrough Common, married, 2 children
Joseph Hawley (?), married, 1 child
Patrick McCourt (?), Barnsley, single
Benjamin Hoyland (60), Worsbrough Dale, married, 1 child
Robert Farrington (?) Oxterly Dyke
William Porter (35), Worsbrough Dale, married, 5 children
William James Porter (12), his son
John Hartley (40), Worsbrough Common, widower, 1 child
John Hartley (12), his son
Walter Hartley (14), his son
James Ellis (31), Worsbrough Bridge, single
John Ellis (37), Worsbrough Bridge, married, 2 children

Walter Ellis (17), his son
Charles Frobisher (39), Worsbrough Dale, married, 3 children
Robert Oldfield (26), Worsbrough Dale, married, 3 children
Richard Cottle (41), Worsbrough Dale, married, 5 children
Nicholas Cottle (17), his son
John Toulson (21)
John Parkin (28), Worsbrough Dale, married, 1 child
Richard Watson (?), Worsbrough Dale, married, 3 children
Richard Hough (38), Worsbrough Common, married, 2 children
James Eastwood (?), Kitroyd, married, 2 children
William Fielding (33), Barnsley, married, 1 child
John Lister (37), Worsbrough, married, 4 children
Thomas Margison (17), Worsbrough Common
Peter Blacker (40), Worsbrough Dale, married
George Wroe (19), Worsbrough Dale, single
Edward Philips (44), Worsbrough Dale, married, 6 children
George Philips (17), his younger son
Joseph Philips (18), his older son
John Hitchen (22), Worsbrough Dale, married, 1 child
George Baker (20), Worsbrough Dale, single
Joseph Walker (35), Worsbrough Common, married, 2 children
Walter Lockwood (23), married, 2 children
James Davies (?)
John Schofield (27), Worsbrough Dale, married, 1 child
George Pickering* (?), Worsbrough Dale, married, 8 children
William Davey* (?), Worsbrough Common, married, 1 child
* got out of the pit alive, died later

Such fatality lists remind us that mining was often a family occupation, a father employing and working with one or more sons. It must have been a devastating time for households in Worsbrough Dale and Worsbrough Common and especially for those who lost one or more family members. What a horrible situation it must have been for the Hartleys who lost a father and two boys aged twelve and fourteen; and also for the wife of Edward Philips who had lost her husband and two teenage sons. Widowed, probably dependant on parish relief, she now had six surviving children to look after.

Conditions of work – as well as working practices – in many South Yorkshire pits at this time were extremely dangerous. Add a dose of bad or irresponsible management or ownership and it was a sure recipe for the occurrence of a serious accident. The risk was high and the number of casualties often a matter of luck. Several smaller 'disasters' underlined the growing importance of a more effective mines' inspection service and an urgent need for legislation. A few months before Edmunds there were six fatalities in a Newton Chambers Company mine, near Sheffield. The pit was known to be 'fiery' but miners were allowed to use candles for light. At the inquest the mines inspector, Charles Morton, informed the jury that the air in the pit was so bad that an anemometer 'would not turn'. The workings furthest away from the shaft had 'no air'. The coroner issued a reprimand and recommended prosecution before the usual 'accidental death' verdict. Then, a year later, in 1863, at Thrybergh Hall Colliery, near Rotherham six men and boys were killed in a terrible accident when they were flung to the bottom of the 150 yard shaft when the descending 'chair' overturned. Another winding accident took place at Wharncliffe Silkstone Colliery on 30 November 1865 when three men were killed when descending the pit, the cage rope having snapped.

In the eyes of the national press Barnsley, now the acknowledged centre of the South Yorkshire coalfield, had also become the country's 'mine disaster capital', an unenviable but sadly accurate appellation which was confirmed on a black December day in 1866 when the Oaks Colliery exploded yet again – with unprecedented human consequences.

Part Five

Valley of Tears
The Oaks Explodes Again,
and Again . . .
1866

'Hoyle Mill is almost entirely bereft of its male population . . . not only has every house one dead, but many two or three, and several four and five . . . A married man named Wilkinson, residing at Darton, has perished with four of his sons.'
Barnsley Chronicle, 15 December 1866

Gloria Victis

(16) Pit: Oaks Colliery

Location: Hoyle Mill, Barnsley
Type: Explosion
Fatalities: 361
Date: Wednesday 12/Thursday 13 December 1866

Estimates have varied over time, but the total number of men, boys and rescue workers killed in this terrible tragedy is now generally accepted to be 361. At the time it was the worst pit disaster in the world. There was no comparable record of sudden, mass death in peacetime Britain, apart from the almost contemporary Sheffield Flood of 1864, when the Dale Dyke Reservoir at Bradfield burst one of its embankments, drowning 250 people. Newspapers of the day compared the Oaks with biblical or classical scourges – even with bloody Culloden. There was just no precedent. The scale and depth of mourning was incomprehensible. Small, tight-knit communities lost virtually their entire young and adult male residents. The Oaks remained as Britain's worst mining disaster, until the Universal Colliery, Senghenydd, near Caerphilly in South Wales, exploded in 1913, with a death-toll of 439. Three years earlier, at the Hulton company's Pretoria pit, in Lancashire, 344 men and boys were killed *on a single day*, four more than in the first explosion at the Oaks. But the second explosion, on 12 December, in which twenty-seven volunteer rescue workers died, pushed the Oaks figure to 361.

We have already seen that the Oaks had already had an unhappy history, and it appears to have been generally regarded as one of the most dangerous pits in South Yorkshire. Many of the men there were concerned about their own safety. On 20 June

An early sketch of the Oaks colliery. A framed version of this was on the wall of a room in a cottage at Hoyle Mill occupied by a descendant of one of the Oaks' victims when I visited them in 1969. Author's collection

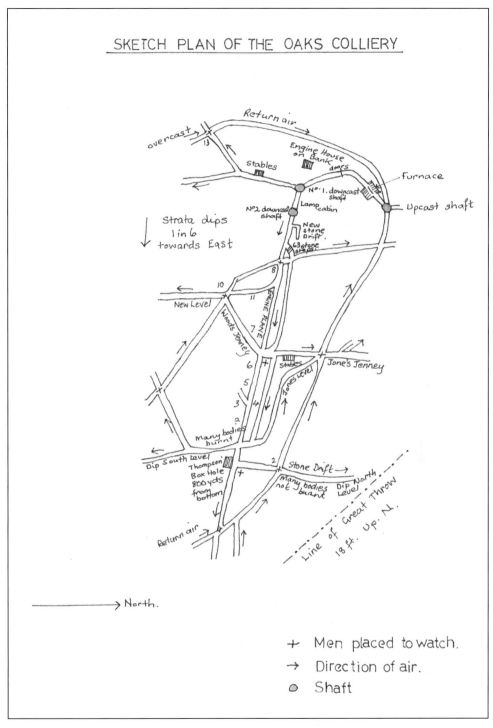

SKETCH PLAN OF THE OAKS COLLIERY

Return air

overcast

Engine House on Bank

stables

doors

Furnace

Nº 1. downcast shaft

Upcast shaft

Nº 2. downcast shaft

Lamp cabin

New stone Drift.

Strata dips 1 in 6 towards East

63 stone steps.

ENGINE PLANE

New Level

Woods Jenney

Stables

Jone's Jenney

Jones Level

Many bodies burnt

Dip South level

Thompson Box Hole 800 yds from bottom

Stone Drift

Many bodies not burnt

Dip North Level

Line of Great Throw 18 ft. up. N.

Return air

North.

+   Men placed to watch.

→   Direction of air.

○   Shaft

Sketch plan showing the extensive underground workings of the Oaks colliery at the time of the 1866 disaster. Brian Elliott

1856, the entire workforce of around 400 withdrew their labour because of 'a fear which has of late come over the miners of accidents being caused by the alleged incompetence of their resident manager'. This was two years before a properly organised miners' union was formed in Yorkshire, when fraternal organisation and representation was weak. Earlier, owners such as Earl Fitzwilliam had issued instructions whereby any of his mineworkers who joined the colliers' union were to be dismissed and therefore made homeless. The district inspector of mines refuted the complaints of the Oaks men but their concerns were such that most of them remained on strike for ten weeks, only returning because of starvation – and the prospect of ejection from their homes. The men's concerns were, of course, well founded. A serious discharge of gas had occurred in 1851. Referring to this incident, in a paper published in 1858, John Brown, a former Oaks viewer (engineer) concurred that 'no amount of ventilation . . . would prevent an explosion, either at the naked lights of the workmen, or at the furnace . . . when firedamp issues in such quantities . . . '. Two further emissions of gas took place in 1857, the year of the Lundhill tragedy. In the spring of 1858 a new furnace was installed, improving the underground flow of ventilation and, for several years, the Oaks was relatively free from firedamp. However, relations between 'masters and men' reached crisis proportions in a bitter dispute during 1864. Blackleg labour was placed under police guard and the striking miners and their families were expelled from colliery-owned houses, many of them barely surviving in tented 'accommodation'. Workmen were evicted by Yorkshire colliery companies in similar circumstances at Denaby Main in 1869, 1885 and 1902; and at Kinsley in 1905.

Fire and smoke: Wednesday 12 December

There were about 340 men and boys (and forty horses) in the Oaks Colliery by lunchtime on 12 December 1866, from a total workforce of around 450. This information was provided by the miners' union. The pit's management did not keep a proper daily record. The underground workforce consisted of a substantive 5.30 am day-shift, plus a small gang of men who had descended at noon. There were few absentees. Wednesday was traditionally regarded as 'make-up day' when the miners strove to maximise their week's pay, especially with Christmas looming. George Cotton and George Ibbotson did not descend the pit with their tools on the fateful day, the latter, very fortuitously, said to have 'laid in bed too long'. Another man, William Wards, was absent, having gone to Chesterfield on union business. Two other fortunate escapees were William Hutchinson and John Outram who ascended the pit a few minutes before the explosion because of damage to a tramway; and also very lucky were the underground steward and his deputies who had come out to have their lunch at the surface. The colliers numbered 131, each assisted by one or two hurriers whose job it was to move the tubs of extracted coal. Horse or pony-drivers, roadway repair men, lamp-cleaners and boys who assisted with the haulage or worked as door-trappers, completed the main underground workforce. Many of them lived nearby, in small tight-knit communities at Hoyle Mill, Measboro' Dyke and Stairfoot. Some walked the mile or so from Barnsley; others lived in the nearby villages of Ardsley, Monk Bretton, Dodworth and a few got up extremely early in order to travel from more distant locations.

The pit exploded at 1.20 in the afternoon, less than an hour before the end of the morning shift. Reporters from the local press were quickly at the scene. The man from the *Barnsley Chronicle* described the immediate aftermath of the blast:

The report was followed by a terrific, and tremendous rush of air, soot, debris, and fragments of wood up the shaft. The convulsion shook the whole neighbourhood, as if the earth had been rent by an earthquake, and was accompanied by a tremendous roar as of distant thunder, but heavier and more terrific. The shock was felt at Hoyle Mill, and also by the inhabitants of houses situated on Doncaster and Pontefract Roads . . . while the report . . . carried the entire intelligence to the distance of over three miles radiating in all directions from the pit. The sound . . . like that from a suddenly agitated volcano, was not to be mistaken, and in less time than we have taken to write these words, the scene on the roads leading to the pit was one which may be concerned, but which language is utterly powerless to describe . . . Here was a wife and mother . . . half running, half walking . . . with a babe in her arms and dragging a young one by the hand; while another who had left them in the care of a neighbour, rushed wildly along, heedless of obstructions . . .

The force of the explosion was so powerful that fine coal dust was deposited on a farm five miles distant.

Relatives at the pit-hill were joined by 'a large number of tradesmen of the town', and

Volunteer rescue workers carry out the dead from the affected workings, a typical scene following Victorian pit disasters. www.cmhrc.co.uk

a messenger was sent to Barnsley so that 'a relay of police' and medical assistance could be obtained. When contacted, Superintendent Greenhalgh dispatched his entire force of ten or twelve officers and four 'medical gentlemen' were soon in attendance. The pit-hill scene was described in typical Victorian melodramatic prose by the *Chronicle* reporter, now an eyewitness to the developing tragedy:

> *The pen of a Dickens would come short of adequately describing the wild excitement which prevailed; the pencil of a Hogarth would fail to portray upon canvas the agony depicted upon the features of the frantic women and children; Shakespeare never wrote, and the greatest tragic actors never displayed upon the stage a scene such as was there witnessed in actual – too actual - reality. One or two sufferers alive but dreadfully scorched had been got out . . . Here was one poor fellow swathed in flannel lifted into a cab just as we arrived. He was black as the coal in his working, the hair was almost entirely singed off his head, his body was frightfully blistered, and his hands and arms were almost completely skinned. His cries, on the cold air reaching his skinned and blistered body when a portion of his wrapper fell off, were excruciating beyond conception, and he was immediately recognised by a female – probably his wife – who in agony of horror screamed, 'Oh, my poor lad! my dear lad, oh dear! oh dear!'*

The cage in the No. 2 downcast shaft had been 'blown away' and the one at the adjacent No. 1 shaft was smashed and its rope broken; and there was slight damage to the winding engine. A new cage was hurriedly put in place and, at 2 pm, forty-five minutes after the explosion the pit manager, Mr Dymond, David Tewart (deputy viewer/engineer) and Christopher Siddons were able to descend the shaft. Twenty men, 'scorched and much affected by the afterdamp' were found in the pit bottom and conveyed to the surface. Many others showed no signs of life: fathers and sons in each other's arms; boys by the side of their ponies; a half-naked collier found with his shirt stuffed into his mouth. Thirty-eight men were found, linked together in each other's arms. They had rushed from their working places and combined to walk towards safety, only to be overtaken by the deadly afterdamp.

The brave work of the rescue workers and fluctuating emotions of the crowd were described in the *Barnsley Chronicle* report:

> *The cage is at the bottom and now the click of the signal wire announces that someone wishes to ascend. Instantly, the pulley wheel revolves . . . eager eyes watch its revolutions, while those on the bank keep their eyes firmly fixed upon the mouth of the shaft, and there is a rush on the part of those behind, which the police with all their vigilance are unable to check. It reaches the level and four or five of the volunteers, half stupefied with the fumes, stagger out. 'Have they brought out any bodies?' is the cry and instantly there is a response of 'Yes' and a stretcher containing a half-shrouded corpse is lifted gently off the bottom of the cage. It is removed under the lights, one of the medical men glances at the stiffened features and glazed eyes of the dead. The name passes from mouth to mouth and instantly there is a cry which indicates the presence of a bereaved one.*

By 4 pm a total of eighty-one bodies had been brought out, including twenty individuals 'barely alive'. Only six of these survived. They were named as Bates, Hart, Marshall, Tasker, Thompson and Youle. Hart had the misfortune to be killed in a later colliery accident. It was soon appreciated that virtually the entire labour force that had descended the pit were dead. *The Times* compared the *(Text continues on page 104)*

The shattered cage 'hanging with a thread' from the broken headstocks at the Oaks colliery following the second explosion. www.cmhrc.co.uk/author's collection

All the drama of the second explosion at the Oaks, one of the most spectacular images ever to be completed of a mine disaster scene. Author's collection/Illustrated London News

People walking towards the disaster scene at the Oaks colliery. Illustrated London News / Author's collection

(continued from page 100) carnage to that experienced in 'a pitched battle' but with even more dire social consequences because 'married men are far more numerous among miners than among soldiers'.

In those days there was no official rescue system. It was to be another thirty-six years before the first mines' rescue station was opened, at Tankersley, near Barnsley. Despite the imminent threat of a further explosion, there were plenty of brave volunteers, including the usual presence of neighbouring mining engineers. Many of the latter arrived at the pit within a few hours of the blast, notably John Brown, WA Potter, P Cooper, and Messrs Smith (from Lundhill), Huntriss, Kell, Maddison, Minto, Platts and Wilson. A Mr Smith, all the way from Durham, also assisted.

One of the first rescue volunteers was one of the deputies who had fortuitously come out of the pit just before it fired. Overcome by grief, he described the loss of his two sons. He found one of them, dead and badly disfigured, lying by the side of his pony. The animal was also dead, burnt, with two of its legs broken. He carried the lad to the pit bottom, ascended the shaft and then returned to search for the body of his other son.

'THE OAKS PIT IS ON FIRE. COME DIRECTLY.' This was the content of the dramatic telegram dispatched to the Derby office of the well-known mining engineer, Thomas Woodhouse. The recipient was on business in London so the message was forwarded to his able partner, Parkin Jeffcock. After what would be his last meal with his parents, at Duffield, Derbyshire, Jeffcock caught a train to Barnsley and arrived at the stricken pit between nine and ten on the night of the disaster. Jeffcock took charge of the search operations which now concentrated on making the pit as safe as possible, including the restoration of the ventilation system. After descending one of the drawing shafts Jeffcock met several of the engineers at the bottom, including Brown, Cooper and Platts who were about to ascend following a long stint underground.

Grey Dawn: Thursday 13 December

At about 1.30 am George Minto was startled in the colliery office when several of the volunteers rushed out of the pit, fearful of an imminent explosion. Minto, a former Oaks engineer, now acting for Mount Osborne and Agnes Road Collieries, had been assisting with the pit-top operations since the previous afternoon. Along with Smith of Lundhill he decided to go down the shaft in order to investigate the problem but found that the alarm was false. But they found the pit's underground engineer, David Tewart and some other men in the lamp cabin and enquired as to the whereabouts of Parkin Jeffcock. The latter was said to have been 'at the bottom of the Engine Plane, repairing an overcast in the Stone Drift level'. On finding Jeffcock the extent of the repair work could be seen, along with many dead bodies, all 'uninjured' but choked by the afterdamp. Gas was still present in considerable quantities, in and near this location.

Frantic filling of tubs with rock in the hope of blocking the cupola shaft at the Oaks following the second explosion. Illustrated London News/Author's collection

At 3 am Jeffcock asked Minto if any explorers were still left in the pit. The reply being negative, Minto was instructed to ascend the shaft and send down the best men he could find so that the dead could be recovered. It was now between 5 and 6 am. Writing later, John Thomas Jeffcock, Parkin Jeffcock's brother, described what happened next:

> Mr Jeffcock sent Christopher Siddons and William Sugden to look at the bottom of Woods Jinney and see if the air was passing up and through the overcast they had last visited; and while he was giving these direction and looking at the colliery plan, Minto said to him 'Had I better not go up now – it is past five – and send the men down?'. Without raising his eyes from the plan, Jeffcock replied, 'Please', and Minto went up the pit bank.

Deputies urged Jeffcock to get out of the pit, to get some food and rest but he refused. He wrote a note for a telegram to be sent to Woodhouse's viewers, Mammatt and Pilkington to come to the pit and inscribed another to Mr Carr, the clerk in the colliery office which read: 'Please arrange with Mr Dymond for the temperatures to be taken of the upcast pit.'

Fresh volunteers entered the pit, as requested by Jeffcock and by 8 am there were about seventy of them underground. Another panic occurred, an explosion perhaps imminent, so sixteen men crammed themselves into a cage which normally accommodated six and were hauled back to safety. They had experienced a 'suck' or reversal of air. Another packed cage-full of men ascended. Sugden, a senior Oaks deputy, remained below. There must have been a great deal of consternation in the pit bottom area, the men there trying to take shelter, some even bidding each other goodbye.

Unable to locate Jeffcock and other volunteers, Minto ascended the shaft at about 8.50 am; then, with Messrs Dymond, Brown, Potter and Smith walked over to the top of the upcast shaft, leaning over to inspect and measure the state of the ascending air. On doing this for a second time there was a great explosion, air rushing up the upcast and downcasts. Minto was knocked backwards with the force of the blast but was not seriously injured. It was 9 am. At No. 1 shaft the cage was blasted into the headgear where it could be seen, shattered and hanging 'with a thread'.

Disbelief, shock and horror permeated the crowd assembled at the pit bank. Strong men 'cried like children', reported the *Barnsley Chronicle* whose man described the terrible scene:

> A momentary stupor seemed to fall upon everyone . . . and for a while all power of action was paralysed. Strong men cried like children . . . and although it was hoping against hope it was suggested that some might have survived the awful occurrence.

There were similar reactions from people returning to the pit, here described by an eyewitness reported in the *Sheffield and Rotherham Independent*:

> I was within 440 yards of the colliery, and within full sight of the buildings . . . when suddenly I was startled with a cry of a man in front of me. It was a cry of the wildest alarm, and looking up I saw, turned on me the face of a pitman, white and horror striken. 'It's fired again', he gasped from his trembling lips, but ere his words had left his mouth, the air was rent with an awful sound. It was a dull, muffled, long continued boom . . . immense black clouds came out of the cupola shaft. I was passing a row of cottages, when suddenly . . . the doors of all were thrown open, and from each there rushed screaming women.

The cage was lowered down but when it ascended it was empty and 'dripping wet'. Two men lay with their heads over the abyss, their shouts echoing and re-echoing but there was no response. The attempt was repeated, everyone at the top in complete silence but the result was the same. Twenty-eight volunteer rescue workers led by Jeffcock seemed to have lost their lives in the second explosion. Despite the great danger of any immediate exploration, one man, Thomas Dawson of Hoyle Mill, offered his services but while he was waiting for a companion to assist the pit exploded yet again. The third explosion, described as 'less violent' than the second, occurred about 7.40 pm. Hope had evaporated. Flames issued from the No. 2 downcast shaft, shooting high into the night air. The entire site was under threat, so spectators were moved towards a bridge, several hundred yards away. The pit's ventilation system was in ruins. Nothing could be done other than wait until dawn.

Meanwhile a telegram from Windsor Castle had arrived at the colliery. It read:

THE QUEEN DESIRES TO MAKE INQUIRY AS TO THE POSSIBLE EXTENT OF THE EXPLOSION, AND WHETHER THE LOSS OF LIFE IS AS SERIOUS AS REPORTED.

The Oaks was a national disaster, attracting a massive amount of publicity and public interest. Among the distinguished visitors to the pit following the second explosion were Earl Fitzwilliam, Lord Wharncliffe, Viscount Halifax (Lord Lieutenant for the West Riding), Major Waterhouse (MP for Pontefract) as well as clergymen from all denominations. JT Woodhouse arrived on site only to find that there was no hope in finding his fellow engineer and business partner Parkin Jeffcock alive.

As if to emphasise the very unstable and dangerous state of the pit, it fired yet again, for the fourth time, at 10.30 pm. Flames could be seen bursting from the shafts, though by the time the Barnsley Fire Brigade had arrived the fire had subsided. With no prospect of any imminent exploration of the workings, certainly no hope of finding anyone still alive, the pit remained quiet and almost deserted during the night.

A miraculous rescue: Friday 13 December
One of the most extraordinary rescues in coal mining history took place at the Oaks Colliery during the early hours of Friday morning, 13 December 1866. According to the *Barnsley Chronicle* 15 December, at about 4 am a few men on the pit hill thought that they could hear a faint noise coming from the bottom of No. 1 shaft. This was not thought to be credible. But at about 4.30 am the signal bell from the same shaft rang. It seemed unbelievable that someone could still be alive and was able to 'call' for help. Men lent over and anxiously shouted downwards but there was no reply. The most senior police officer on duty, Inspector Weatherall of Wakefield sent a message to the mining engineers who were staying at the King's Head, Barnsley, about a mile away. When they arrived the first course of action to be tried was to attach a bottle containing brandy and water to a rope and lower it down the shaft. When the vessel was extracted it was empty, so clearly someone below was still alive. The big question was now what to do in order to execute a rescue. There was no cage or normal winding system operational. A makeshift pulley was set up and an iron bucket or sinking tub attached to a chain. Power to use this equipment was provided by steam from a small saw mill engine, a fire having been hurriedly started. John Edward Mammatt, the site engineer in charge – volunteered to descend the pit, riding in the bucket. Woodhouse asked for another volunteer, someone of light weight stature. A young man, Thomas Embleton, came forward, permission then being sought from his father for him to go down. One report describes the bucket as being so small that each man could only place one foot inside, the other

hanging in the darkness. They sheltered their safety lamps from the water under their clothes, using their other hand to cling onto the rope. After about 150 yards of descent both men got soaked with water bursting on them from broken 'cribs' at the side of the shaft. The sound from this was so loud that they were unable to hear any further instructions. It probably took at least fifteen minutes for the bucket to reach the bottom where there was an additional danger – a sump full of deep water. Precariously advancing a few yards along the roadway the intrepid volunteers found Samuel Brown sitting on a pile of rubbish. The latter was unable to give any coherent replies to questions regarding any other survivors, saying, 'Take me out, take me out.' As Mammatt placed his own foot into the bucket it keeled over and threw him into the sump but he was able to save himself from drowning by clutching onto an iron bar. The apparatus somehow containing all three men was raised to the surface, rather faster than the descent. Samuel Brown had been in the pit for almost 24 hours. He was taken to one of the colliery's sheds 'where restoratives were administered'. Brown was now able to describe some of the

This kibble or sinking bucket, on display at the National Mining Museum for England, is believed to have been the one used by Mammatt and Embleton in their successful rescue of Samuel Brown. Contemporary reports, however, refer to what seems to be a smaller vessel. Photo: Brian Elliott

circumstances relating to his remarkable survival. He was resting with three of his colleagues in the lamp-room when the second explosion occurred. After recovering from a period of unconsciousness, his friends apparently dead, he made his way to the pit bottom of No 2 shaft, sat down and thought to himself: 'This will not do; I must seek summat'. He then made his way through the darkness, stumbling over dead bodies, to No 1 shaft and rang the signal bell. He further stated that he heard no-one moaning and that there was 'not a living thing' left in the pit. Mammatt and Embleton had performed an act of extreme bravery, risking their own lives in the process.

Early on Saturday morning another explosion occurred, followed by a further thirteen over the next three days. A decision was made to seal the mine by filling all three shafts at strategic points, a process that continued well into January 1867. Measurements of air pressure and temperature was facilitated by means of a pipe inserted into the No 2 shaft. This also allowed gas to escape.

Sightseeing, mourning and the recovery of bodies

Large crowds of sightseers visited the Oaks Colliery site on 16 December 1866, the first Sunday following the disaster. Special train excursions ran to Barnsley from Sheffield, Leeds, Wakefield and Manchester. Normally quiet roads near the pit became a conglomeration of people and assorted vehicles. Impromptu open-air religious services were held amid the busy scene. The Bishop of Ripon had a very busy day, preaching about the disaster at special services held in Barnsley's principal churches: St Mary's, St John's and St George's.

Burial of those bodies which had been recovered took place at Ardsley, Monk Bretton and in the spacious newly-opened Barnsley cemetery. 'Wailings and lamentations' dominated the sad scene at Ardsley churchyard when thirty-five bodies were interred in a mass grave. The monument subsequently placed there, financed by public subscription, also commemorates all miners killed in the disaster. Horse-drawn hearses passed through Barnsley town centre, trailed by long processions of black-clothed mourners, walking with unconcealed emotion. Presided over by the Bishop of Ripon, thirty-five bodies were buried in separate graves in Barnsley cemetery. One spectator, a man called Rothwell, lost control and had to be forcibly removed from the scene.

It was a grim Christmas in the shattered community of Hoyle Mill. Many bereaved families had to wait many months, even years before the body of a loved one was recovered. In 1969 I interviewed Mrs Northrop, aged 85, who lived in Beevor Street. The body of her uncle, eighteen-year-old Thomas Cooper, was recovered three years after the disaster, identified by his water bottle. Almost all households lost one or more inhabitants. Few males between the ages of twelve and sixty could be seen. Oak Row was typical. Of the eleven households nine were directly affected by the disaster:

House	Fatality	Age	Dependants
1	George Addy	33	Wife
2	Walter Hawley	19	Mother (a widow) and seven children; Walter was the breadwinner
3	Thomas Hyde	25	Wife and 2 children
4	Aaron Sissons	34	Wife and 3 children
5	Thomas Leather	30	Wife and 4 children
6	Joseph Ball	34	Wife and 5 children
	Thomas Ball	16	Son of Thomas
7	Thomas Wood	28	Wife and 3 children
8	William Sugden	-	Wife and 3 children
9	Robert Rimmington	18	Single

I also interviewed a descendant of Thomas Hyde. A pit-sinker, he came to live at Hoyle Mill from Swadlincote, Derbyshire, finding employment at the Oaks just six months before disaster struck. His body was recovered on 16 June 1868, identified by a darned patch on his trousers. William Sugden was the underground steward.

Along Ash Row the devastation was even greater. On the morning of Sunday 16 December all but one of thirty households had its curtains drawn, the exception being the policeman's.

In Hoyle Mill there were about sixty houses. From these, 103 men and boys were

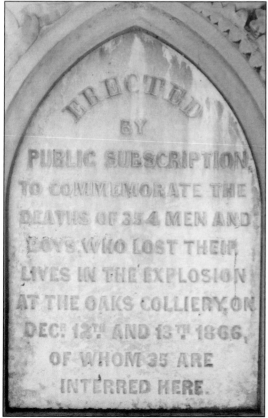

Above left: *The Oaks memorial in Ardsley churchyard as it appeared, before restoration, in 1969.* Photo: Brian Elliott

Above right: *The Oaks memorial today. There are also several extant individual memorials to Oaks victims nearby.* Photo: Brian Elliott

Left: *Detail of the inscription, completed at a time when the exact number of fatalities was not certain.* Photo: Brian Elliott

This page and opposite: *Cottages at Hoyle Mill where many Oaks colliery miners lived, photographed by the author in 1969. They still exist in 2006, most with new window frames and a good number of satellite dishes fixed to the exterior walls.*

killed in the Oaks, leaving 167 widows and 366 children under the age of twelve. A fifty per cent depopulation had occurred in one afternoon.

The terrible task of the recovery of bodies was a slow and painful process. After the shafts were re-opened the first body – that of John James, one of the rescue workers – was found on 25 September 1867. He was identified by the sole of his boot and part of his waistcoat. A few days later the bodies of David Tewart and William Sugden were recovered. Tewart was described as 'almost entirely uninjured . . . his long flowing beard not so much as singed'. Sugden's funeral at Dodworth was a grand affair, attended by thirty surviving Oaks miners and 113 widows.

There was great excitement at the pit bank on 4 October 1867 when, following the extraction of the remains of Alfred Hoyland, a notebook belonging to Parkin Jeffcock was found. The bodies of John Smith, Lundhill's mining engineer, and the Oaks' steward Christopher Siddons were also retrieved, the former identified by his pocket watch. An estimated crowd of 4,500 was present at Smith's funeral in Barnsley cemetery, including the entire workforce of Lundhill Colliery. Jeffcock was also found, very badly mutilated, his name-tag on his shirt collar. He was buried at Ecclesfield.

Sixty bodies were recovered during 1868, many of them recognised by items of clothing or possessions. Another forty-seven were got out during the first eight months of 1869. The terrible work was always under the threat of further explosions, as happened on 5 December 1869 when there were three.

An unusual incident took place in Barnsley Cemetery on 3 May 1868 when several Oaks men were being buried, some of them in a mass grave. The widows were angry, one of them shouting: 'They are burying him like a dog . . . shame . . . shove the one with the white gown (the presiding parson) in.' The frightened cleric had to be escorted away by several police officers.

The author obtained this photograph, printed from a glass negative, of Mrs Hyde an Oaks widow when he visited a descendant of the family in 1969. Her husband, Thomas was a pit sinker and had come to the Oaks from Swadlincote, Derbyshire. His body was not recovered until eighteen months after the disaster. Mrs Hyde identified him from a patch that she had darned on his pit trousers. The couple were both aged 25 and had two young children. It is impossible to fully appreciate the impact of mining disasters on families but personal stories such as this certainly help. Brian Elliott

The new cemetery at Barnsley was the scene of large crowds during the funerals of the Oaks victims in 1866, many of them interred without any headstone. The obelisk in the foreground is to the memory of John Smith, one of the young mining engineers and rescue workers killed in the second explosion. Photo: Brian Elliott, 2006

The John Smith memorial, photographed by the author in 1969.

IN MEMORY
OF
JOHN SMITH,
UNDERVIEWER AT THE
LUNDHILL COLLIERY,
WHO LOST HIS LIFE IN
THE OAKS EXPLOSION
WHILST EXPLORING WITH
A PARTY OF VOLUNTEERS
ON THE 13TH DECEMBER
1866, AGED 36 YEARS.

"BOAST NOT THYSELF
OF TO MORROW: FOR THOU
KNOWEST NOT WHAT A DAY
MAY BRING FORTH."
PROV. XXVII.

THIS MONUMENT IS ERECTED
BY A FEW FRIENDS WHO DEEPLY
REGRET HIS LOSS.

ALSO OF MARGARET

Detail of the main inscription of the John Smith memorial. Photo: Brian Elliott

Widows would flock to the pit whenever news reached them that human remains had been found. There was a very unexpected further fatality: a Miss Newsome visited the pit out of curiosity but got tangled in some machinery, later dying from her injuries.

When giving evidence to the Royal Commission of 1881, John Edward Mammatt, one of the heroes of the Oaks disaster stated that eighty bodies were still unaccounted for, still entombed in the pit. Sentiment from the new generation of Oaks pitmen soon waned in favour of a more practical approach:

> *We sometimes come across some bones, we did the other day, and we sent them up to the top, but nobody claimed them, and they were buried; there was only a skull and a piece of leg bone.*

Families in need of relief

The public response towards supporting dependants was immediate. Another telegram from Queen Victoria arrived on Friday 14 December 1866, the day following the second fatal explosion. Her Majesty expressed her regret concerning the 'frightful calamity' and promised £200 'if a subscription is set on foot . . . for the relief of the families of the unfortunate sufferers'. The Lord Mayor of London opened a subscription list at the Mansion House for the widows and children of those killed and £10,000 was raised within two weeks. Similar gestures resulted in funds being established in Sheffield, Leeds, Doncaster, Huddersfield, Hull, Liverpool, Wigan, Edinburgh and many other locations. Examples of the many small sums sent by named and anonymous individuals and organisations were listed in the Yorkshire press. Entries such as 'The commercial gentleman dining at the Royal Hotel [Barnsley] on Thursday – £2'; 'G' – five shillings; 'A friend – five shillings', were typical. The small North Yorkshire village of Thornton, near Pickering donated £25.

Locally, a few days after the disaster, on 17 December, a meeting was convened at Barnsley's Court House in order to establish a public subscription fund. Victorian society was already notable for raising money for a wide variety of civic projects, memorials, and for war and disaster relief. A detailed report of proceedings appeared in the next edition of the *Barnsley Chronicle*, published on 22 December.

The meeting proved to be far from harmonious. Its chairman was Earl Fitzwilliam, Lord Lieutenant of the West Riding, well-known for his mining interests but, as we have seen, no friend of the miners' union. The platform included some of the bewhiskered establishment of the day: Lord Wharncliffe, Viscount Halifax, Viscount Milton, J Spencer-Stanhope, TW Wentworth, TE Taylor (district coroner), TE Bower plus an assortment of MPs and clerics headed by the Archbishop of York.

Earl Fitzwilliam was the first of the elite to enter the hall and was greeted with 'loud cheers' by the waiting assembly. After the formal opening, the Archbishop put forward the following motion:

> *That this meeting has heard with heartfelt regret the frightful calamity that occurred at the Oaks Colliery on Wednesday last, when upwards of three hundred lives were sacrificed by an explosion, and records its deepest sympathy with the widows and orphans of the sufferers.*

Lord Wharncliffe, also welcomed by 'cheers', spoke in support of the Archbishop's opening remarks. Then matters turned somewhat contentious when Reverend Day

Barnsley Court House was used for what turned out to be a most controversial public meeting which established a relief fund for the Oaks victims' families. It was also the venue of the adjourned inquest. Photographed in 1969. Brian Elliott

ventured a second motion, largely in support of the Oaks colliery's owners. His proposal was as follows:

> *That this meeting further expresses its cordial sympathy with the proprietors of the Oaks Colliery, not simply because of the great loss of property entailed, but by the crushing sorrow endured by the terrible loss of lives of their workmen, and the bereavement of those connected with them.*

Day went on to express his admiration of Mr Dymond, the colliery's manager, and commended his ability. Perhaps not surprisingly, T E Taylor, the coroner and friend of Dymond, seconded the motion, saying that the 'agonies he [Dymond] endured were far greater than his loss of property'.

It was at this point that there was a small disturbance from the back of the hall. Reverend Crompton, unable to control himself any longer, sprang to his feet and requested that before Day's resolution was seconded he would like to say a few words. Crompton was invited to move to the front of the room, whereupon he addressed the platform as follows:

> *My Lord, I can not help making this observation. I feel much regret at the necessity for any remark being made upon the resolution which must commend itself to a great degree to our feelings, and, gentlemen, though I feel I have as strong a sympathy with the masters as any man in the room, yet this resolution will express to many in Barnsley a peculiar regret. It will suggest a very painful regret that there has not been provision made before by sinking an adequate number of shafts in other parts of the pit, in order to lesson the danger [cries of 'Hear, hear' at this point] and very probably avert any such calamity as this we now deplore [cries of 'Order! Order!'].*

The plucky Reverend, undeterred, continued:

My Lord, am I in order? [cries of 'No! No!'] I object to the resolution in this form and believe I have the right – as an Englishman – to speak in a public meeting [cries of 'Hear, hear' countered with 'Order! Order!']. My feeling is that . . . however much deep sorrow and sympathy there may be with the masters under this crushing afflication . . . we can not help thinking that if two other shafts had been sunk . . . this calamity might never had occurred [shouts of 'Hear, hear' followed by 'uproar and confusion'].

After the commotion had died down various other speakers objected to Reverend Crompton's 'outburst', saying that he was 'out of order' and it was 'not the meeting's concern'. The chairman, Earl Fitzwilliam, referred to the parson's intervention as opening 'so interminable a field of controversy that there would be no end to the discussion'.

Crompton's brave outburst, no doubt based on his conversations with local miners, highlighted the great social divisions of the day. His alternative motion did not find a seconder.

The meeting continued in a more subdued fashion, with subsequent resolutions praising the bravery of the rescue workers and the generosity of the Queen. The outcome was a committee under Earl Fitzwilliam's chairmanship, established for the guardianship of what was to be called 'The Oaks Colliery Relief Fund'. Local solicitor George Peacock (at a fee of £50 pa) was placed in charge of administration.

Eventually, £48,747 was raised, including a substantial donation of £11,697 from the Lord Mayor of London's Mansion House Fund. Chargeable were 690 individuals comprising 68 men, 248 women and 374 children. In 1908, the capital having fallen to £27,000, the Charity Commissioners formed a trust enabling the fund to be used for the dependants of later local pit disasters. By 1998 just three dependants accessed the fund which had fallen to £16,000 and a report in the *Barnsley Chronicle* of 5 November 1999 said that the charity was to be 'wound up'.

Despite all the fund raising the families of the dead received inadequate support. Many of the deceased would have subscribed to the Oaks accident insurance club but there was no way that it could meet such a sudden huge demand. However, several of the Friendly Societies – subscribed to by many working class families to offset funeral costs – did honour claims. The Barnsley Board of Guardians, however, refused applications of relief on the grounds that the colliery's owners were providing widows with a small amount of temporary financial aid and rent-free accommodation. After protest, the Guardians subsequently agreed to relieve just twenty-six Oaks widows whose only means of support was the disaster fund. They were each given two shillings (10p) a week and one shilling (5p) for every child.

The miners' union did what it could to support the widows and children but its fund could not cope since a substantial proportion of the men who were killed were members. As such, their wives were entitled to £8 for funeral expenses (subject to a body being recovered), five shillings (25p) a week in assistance and one shilling (5p) per week for each dependant child under the age of twelve.

In the wake of the Oaks an unsuccessful attempt was made to form a mutual insurance fund for much of the South Yorkshire Coalfield with 'noblemen and gentlemen' on its committee. In 1867, £2,284 was transferred from the Hartley Colliery Disaster (Northumberland, 1862, over 200 fatalities) Relief Fund but pitmen were not

A young pit lad.
Author's collection

informed about this initiative. It was only after the Swaithe Main disaster of 1875 (see below) that a proper miners' relief fund was established (known as the West Riding of Yorkshire Miners' Permanent Relief Fund).

The inquest and report

On the same day as Brown's remarkable rescue the inquest opened at the Old White Bear, Hoyle Mill on 14 December, before the local coroner, Mr T Taylor. Fifteen jurors, all male, were sworn in and sixteen bodies were identified. Further sittings took place at Barnsley Court House, beginning on 20 December.

Evidence was heard over a period of thirteen days with much discussion, though no definite conclusion as to the cause of the explosion. However, there was abundant testimony from individual miners to show that gas was present in both old and current workings during the hours and days before the disaster. It was also evident that a deputation of Oaks miners had complained to the management about the dangerous state of some of the workings only two weeks earlier. Charles Morton, the overworked district mines' inspector undertook a lot of the questioning but resigned after the second day of the adjourned inquest. Although said to be suffering from chronic rheumatism, the prospect of reporting on yet another major disaster had an enormous impact on his mental health. The task of providing further evidence to the inquest and then writing what must have been a daunting official report was passed to his colleague, Joseph Dickinson, the Lancashire inspector.

A great deal of discussion surrounded the fact that the first explosion took place at the same time as blasting operations in a new stone drift. However, most of the expert witnesses would not accept this as a cause largely because of the distance that the gas would have had to travel from the workings. Dickinson also considered that it was unlikely that ignition was caused from a faulty or unlocked safety lamp since he considered the pit to be well-managed. Some of the engineers were of the opinion that coal could have been better worked 'in districts' (compared with the long-wall or 'Barnsley' method) which could have, theoretically speaking, limited the extent of any explosion.

With regard to the view that the Oaks would have had better ventilation by means of the sinking of more shafts, this was ruled out by the engineers on the grounds of expense. Human lives were cheap in comparison.

The Old White Bear (now the Hoyle Mill Inn) which was used for the inquest on the bodies of the first Oaks victims. Photographed in 1969. Brian Elliott

On the final day, Mr Channell, representing the Miners' Association (Union) wanted to call on David Dymond, the pit's manager, to give evidence but this request was turned down. The colliery owners' solicitor, Mr Blackburn, stated that Dymond would only answer questions from the jury. The owners' argument was accepted by the coroner. Thus a key figure in this national disaster did not contribute to the inquest.

The last person to be questioned was the government commissioner, John Kenyon Blackwell, who stated that the evidence did not lead him to form any definite conclusion as to the cause of the accident.

After a 75-minute deliberation the foreman of the jury read out the predictable 'accidental death' verdict:

> That Richard Hunt and others were killed by an explosion of gas or firedamp at the Oaks Colliery on 12 December, but there is no evidence to prove where or how it ignited. The jury think it not necessary to make any special recommendations as to the working of mines, seeing that the government are collecting information, no doubt with a view of the better protection of life, they think a more strict inspection desirable.

Popular reaction to the inquest evidence and verdict included a barrage of condemnation and criticism:

> All we say is, let the truth come out . . . let us know to what we owe this sad disaster, and, not take refuge in the belief that it arose from the neglect of some solitary miner in a distant part of the pit, in damaging his safety lamp amid an atmosphere where a naked light was certain destruction.
> *Sheffield and Rotherham Independent*, 22 December 1866

> The evidence on Monday . . . has strongly confirmed the first (shot- blasting) explanation of the cause of the disaster.
> *The Scotsman*, 8 January 1867

> But it is impossible to avoid the conclusion that for the first week or fortnight before the final catastrophe, the miners at the Oaks Colliery worked with their lives in constant jeopardy . . . There were naked lights in some parts of the mine. Moreover, a process of blasting by gunpowder was going on, and the evidence strongly points this circumstance as the immediate cause of the disaster.
> *London Telegraph*, 7 January 1867

> We do not find fault with the evidence being taken, but we do say that it ought to have been rendered before another tribunal, one composed of commissioners appointed by the government to enquire into the best mode of working coal in the country.
> *Barnsley Chronicle*, 2 February 1867

> The result is a vague verdict delivered amid a 'feu de joie' of compliments . . . with fruits like this of the cheap system of working seams, which, all the engineers describe as highly dangerous, parliament and public can not hesitate to say that the system must be changed.
> *Sheffield and Rotherham Independent*, 2 February 1867

> Disappointment, we are convinced, will be felt by everybody, except perhaps the managers and owners of the mine, that after all the evidence, the decisions offered to the public are little more than empty platitudes.
> *London Telegraph*, 4 February 1867

Joseph Dickinson's report was submitted to parliament on 26 April 1867. After running a feature on the contents, the *London Telegraph* summed up the general feeling of many:

> *If nine or ten fashionable people were killed at the opera or 364 at the Grand Stand at Epsom, we should find means to obviate the causes of such catastrophes. Let those who make our laws be as much in earnest for the poor miners, upon whom blunted and deadened as they are by their daily peril, it is absurd to rely.*

A separate report which also included a transcript summary of the inquest was published by Kenyon Blackwell. Sadly, the Oaks disaster did not directly influence new mining legislation. Petitions were sent to the Home Office requesting that a Royal Commission should be established to enquire into the Oaks disaster and the dangerous state of the nation's coal mines. Joseph Dickinson and mines' inspector colleagues, along with Mr Matthews, President of the Miner Owners Association were interviewed by a House of Commons select committee. One suggestion was that the mines inspectorate should be increased from twelve to twenty-four. The government did not respond with any urgency and when they did legislation had little or no impact on safety. By the time that the 1872 Coal Mines Act was operational at least a dozen more major explosions had occurred in British coal mines, including a great toll at Pontypridd (178 deaths in 1867 and 53 in 1869). Under the new regulations pit managers were required to have a 'certificate of competence' obtained via a state examination; miners' representatives were allowed to carry out safety inspections and the employment of boys was limited to ten hours per day, with a day's education allowed every two weeks. There was little else.

Gravestone of Thomas Sutcliffe of Hoyland Common who died during the sinking of the New Oaks shaft in 1869. A.K. Clayton/Brian Elliott

Postscript

Even after a great disaster it was rare for a pit not to continue functioning in some form or other. Commercial interest outweighed sentiment. Even while bodies were still being recovered, a new shaft was being sunk nearby, at Stairfoot. In October 1869 one of the New Oaks shafts had reached 130 yards. A year later coal was reached at 334 yards. In 1874 Old and New Oaks collieries were owned by Cammel and Company until closure in about 1910. The site was then occupied by Yorkshire Tar Distillers until that plant closed in 1970.

When I visited the Old Oaks pit bank almost forty years ago it was still possible to see the tops of the old drawing shafts. They really were remarkably small openings for one of the deepest and most extensively worked pits in South Yorkshire. Not long afterwards, the site was obliterated, during the re-development of the Barnsley Main complex. A few rare images survive showing interior features of the shafts, taken during demolition and clearance work. Today, a solitary old NCB pit headgear is the only obvious reminder of former mining activity. However, nearby, at Hoyle Mill, many of the cottages in which Oaks miners lived can still be seen, as can the Old White Bear, where the inquest started.

Unfortunately, there is no public memorial marking the site of England's worst mining disaster, or the eighty or more bodies still entombed in the old workings. However, as we have seen, the mass grave in Ardsley churchyard also pays tribute to the men and boys killed in the disaster. There are of course many individual gravestones. One of the saddest is that dedicated to five of the Winter brothers, aged 17–32. Many of the Oaks victims were buried en masse, in unmarked areas of Barnsley's new

The tops of the two drawing shafts of the Oaks could still be seen, on the Barnsley Main site, in 1969.
Photo: Brian Elliott

Standing near one of the Oaks shafts in 1969 demonstrated how small they were, and yet were used for large numbers of men and many tons of materials. Photo: Brian Elliott

The old pit bank of the Oaks was sited right next to the railway, The later Barnsley Main headstocks can be seen in the background. Photo: Brian Elliott

A section of one of the narrow Oaks drawing shafts was revealed during demolition in c.1972. Author's collection

Perhaps the most tragic family affected by the Oaks disaster were the Winters. This gravestone in Barnsley cemetery lists five brothers, aged 17–32, killed in the disaster.
Photo: Brian Elliott

Victorian cemetery. The impressive *Gloria Victis* monument on Doncaster Road, Kendray was funded in 1912/13 by a local businessman, Samuel Joshua Cooper, saddened by the 1912 Cadeby disaster when more than fifty rescue workers were killed. Now adjacent to new housing and overlooking one of Barnsley's busiest roads, it pays tribute to Parkin Jeffcock 'and other heroes of the rescue parties' who died in the second Oaks explosion; and commemorates the singular bravery of Mammatt and Embleton in 'rescuing the sole survivor'. It does not refer to the 334 miners killed in the 1866 disaster but is often erroneously referred to as 'the Oaks disaster memorial'. TW Embleton, said to be 'the last survivor of rescue parties at the Oaks Colliery', died in 1921. Brown, the man saved by Mammatt and Embleton, became something of a local celebrity, the recipient of complimentary drinks in local pubs and the subject of *The Story of Samuel Brown, the solitary survivor of the rescue party of the Oaks Colliery explosions, December 12*

and 13th 1866, commuted by him to the Reverend J.F.T. Hallows, M.A., Barnsley, one of several opportunistic tracts and booklets published following the disaster.

A number of commemorative items, ranging from funeral or mourning cards to pottery were also produced. A somewhat unusual gesture was the presentation of a commemorative bible by the Oaks Colliery Explosion Relief Fund Committee to a deceased's widow or dependant. Some memorabilia has survived in museums and private collections.

The recording of all miners killed in the disaster was a very difficult task since Barber and Company did not keep a list of their workmen. It was left to John Normansall, the new Secretary of the South Yorkshire Miners' Association and the surviving committee of the Oaks branch of the union to provide an early list of missing men and boys and those recovered, but exclusive of those who were not members. A scroll of 341 'unfor-

In Memory of

Three Hundred and Sixty

MEN AND BOYS,

Killed by the Explosions at the Oaks Colliery, Barnsley,

DECEMBER 12th and 13th, 1866.

Colliers.

Philip Bates
* Andrew Barker, Sen.
Isaac Timmings
Matthew Arnold
John Whitaker
Peter Day
Josh. Watson
David Hallworth
Josh. Leather
Henry Marsden
Josh. Bantam
John Bradley
Fergus Rhodes
Thomas Wood
John Lawley
Thos. Cooper
William Duckett
Thomas Walton
Geo. Gladwin
James Thornley
Samuel Helliwell
Ewd. Kenworthy
Chas. Randerson
Richard Oakley
Wm. Matthews
John Halliwell
Chas. Webb
Daniel Bradley
Walter Hawley
Frederick Fletcher
John Castle
John Edson
Charles Hutchinson
John Bonson
Josh. Mort
William Edson
Samuel Dunk
David Fawcett Simpson
George Sykes
Charles Ramsden
John Bradley
John Evans
Robert Hurst
John Newton
George Addy
James Lane
George Marshall
Henry Wood
Peter McDonald
Richard Clarkson
Fred. Holdsworth
John Nuthall
George Hobson
John Denniss
John Hincheliffe
Charles Clegg
William Rhodes
Samuel Ramsden
Henry Ruthwell
Abraham Dennis
* Andrew Barker, Junior
John Armfield
Abel Cartwright
John Bates
Benjamin Dennis
John Sowden
Thos. Payman
Thos. Hydes
Thos. Taylor
George Damms
William Mattrick
John Winter
George Birchall

John Conley
Duncan Winter
William Abbott
George Evans
George Lawley
Josh. Peaker
Edward Cartwright
Jervis Rider
Edward Musgrave
George Dawsons
Josh. Batty
George Arnold
Thos. Pickles
Thos. Barker *
Josh. Poppleton
Thos. Leather
Thos. Donkin
John Farmer
Josh. Harrison
John Ward
John Brown
Aaron Scissons
George Smith
Charles Brooke
Richard Clapham
Thos. Jones
Hy. Jackson
Josh. Bard
Hy. Poppleton, Junior
William Haigh
Jas. Haycroft
Hy. Hilton
Matthew Balmforth
George Shirt
John Sloane
Charles Connolly
James Bennett
George Coward
John Cartright
Josh. Roebuck
Hy. Hincheliffe
Joshua Faulks
Thos. Winter

Hurriers.

Richard Barker *
Moses Bates
John Smith
Daniel Wall
John Arnold
William Syder
Thos. Highlands
Josh. Hunt
Alfred Smith
Arthur Birkinshaw
William Dodgson
Benjamin Moss
Charles Exley
Mathew Swift
Josh. Lea
George Nadin
George Rhodes
Thos. Bennett
George Ellis
Fred. Smith
Abraham Wilkinson
Thos. Horbury
William Winter
Henry Winter
John McCarthy
Michael Rowning
Thomas Dixon
John Clegg
John Collin
John Moss
William Parker

Solomon Bellamy
Tom Donkin
George Edson
William Wilkinson
David Holland
Benjamin Brown
William Slater
Martin Gilbright
Nathan Race
Thos. Wright
Samuel Holliday
Alfred Brown
Charles Rhodes
George Haylands
David Cooper
Richard Shaw
George Miller
George Wilkinson
William Edson
Josh. Hollin
John Marshall
Thos. Clarke
Henry Gott
William Lee
Jas. Glover
William Wharton
Thomas Ward
Lot Brownlow
Charles Fearn
Henry Ramsden
William Shirt
William Stones
William Barker
Frank Clarkson
Stephen Robinson
William Bates
Charles Brown
John Pooley
Thomas Seddons
William Haworth
George Hitchin
Thomas Henry
Thomas Schofield
George Moore
Josh. Winter
George Carr
William Wright
Josh. Cooper
George Tupman
Henry Hall
George Musgrave
John Richardson
James Batty
William Thompson
Charles Matthews
Henry Osborne
William Barker *
Robert Hackin
Robert Rimmington *
David Fearn
Charles Clary
William Middleton
Matthew Dixon
Charles Harrison
Alfred Barraclough
Josh. Thorpe
Samuel Thorpe
John Shore
Michael McDonald
Thomas Anderson
Alfred Healey
William Sykes
Thomas Glover
John Jones
William Berry
Josh. Smith

George Hoyell
John Edson
Amos Cooke
Thomas Hutchinson
William McLintock
Thomas Bennett
William Jones
Samuel Jones
Benjamin Fairclough
Robert Thornton
Josh. Lee
Walter Hessle
John Pashley
Edward Evans
Henry Clayton
John Exley
John Noble
John Connolly
John Bennett
Andrew Coward
Matthew Roebuck
Charles Hincheliffe
William Boothroyd
Samuel Seddons
Charles Challenger
John Halton

Deputies.

William Sugden
Christopher Seddons
John Robson
William Wilson

Day Men.

Thomas Nadin
Giles Walmsley
Thomas Hammond
John Everett
Edward Seddons
Samuel Richardson
John Willies
Joshua Raynor
Charles Thawley
Henry Brook
John Thompson
Mark Lee
Alfred Hoyland
Benjamin Jowett
George Ibbotson
Jabez Kay
Henry Chesterfield
Thomas Hardcastle
Henry Poppleton
Josh. Keighley
John Warmsley
Richard Hunt
John Clayton
William Dawson
James Barker, Senior *
George Borrodale *
Ephraim Sellars
Matthew Scales
Henry Willowby
George Lover

Day Boys.

John Cadman
John Bates
John McHugh
William Norman
Josh. Priestley
Charles Osborne

John Rooke
John Pickford
Alfred Armitage
Josh. Walker
Austin Lane
John Carr
George Hough
Benjamin Exley
Elijah Slater
Thompson Thickett
James Raynor
Edward Bradley
Andrew Barker
Alfred Poppleton
Thomas Wilson
Thomas Hellowell
William Haigh
James Walmsley
Josh. Senior
Josh. Wilson
Henry Haigh
Thomas Band
Michael Grant
Matthew Allen
John Graham
George Barker, No. 1
Charles Donkin
William Watson
Richard Massey
Ephraim Nadin
John Jackson
William Hill
John Keene
John Hardcastle
William Bates
Matthew Mattrick
Samuel Stenton
George Coldwell
Josh. Bargon
Charles Fletcher
John Hayes
Ezra Illingworth
James Fleetwood
George Poppleton
John Holbrooks
George Barker, No. 2
Thomas Bennett
William Dixon
William Carr
Frederick Payman

Volunteers.

Parkin Jeffcock, Esq.
John Smith, Landhill
David Towart, Underground Viewer
Thomas Stead
James Heading
Robert Hepinstall
Thomas Banks
George Backhouse
William Robinson
Francis Holbeck
Henry Haywood
Henry Beaumont
Thomas Dickenson
Henry Brierley
Robert Hall
Richard Christholme
John James
William Shaw
Samuel Clegg
John Dawson

Several listings of Oaks victims were produced, this example is one of the more accurate versions. The asterisks refer to those who died from the Ingleton area. Northern Mine Research Society

tunate sufferers' and thirteen volunteers was produced by 'a local artist', published in Frank Machin's NUM-sponsored *The Yorkshire Miners* book in 1958. The *Barnsley Chronicle* published a similar listing 'presented gratuitously to every purchaser' in its edition of 23 February 1867. When originally researching the Oaks disaster I compiled a list of fatalities from the parishes of Ardsley and Monk Bretton, including the dates of interment, extracted from church burial registers. These can be seen in the Appendix of my dissertation (see Bibliography) lodged in Barnsley Archives and Local Studies Library.

There are many fateful stories relating to individuals killed in the Oaks disaster. One recently came to my attention, courtesy of Mike Gill of the Northern Mine Research Society. This concerns a small group of men from the Ingleton area who had left their villages in desperate search for work, finding employment in the Barnsley area, at the Oaks Colliery. Most of them lost their lives. They were:

James Barker, aged 51, who left a widow and 6 children
Thomas Barker, 26, son of the above, left a widow and 1 child
Andrew Barker, 19, son of James
William Barker, 16, son of James
Robert Remington, 15
George Borrowdale, 51, widower, left a son and a daughter
Andrew Barker, 46 (from Burton), left a widow and 7 children
Richard Barker, 15, son of the above

Clearly, the impact back home was enormous for the Barker families. By another twist of fate, Robert Remington's father, Richard, escaped death as he had not gone to work on the 12 December because of illness. George Borrowdale was one of the eighteen men brought out of the pit alive immediately after the first explosion but was so badly burnt that he died within a few days. On Friday 14 December a deputation from the Oaks Branch of the South Yorkshire Miners' Association visited the homes of the bereaved families in Ingleton in order to discover the above information.

Part Six

Dull Rumblings, Loud Reports and a Deathly Plunge
1867–1890

'The centuries will burn rich loads
With which we groaned,
Whose warmth shall lull their dreaming lids
While songs are crooned.
But they will not dream of us poor lads
Left in the ground.'

The Miners, Wilfred Owen

A trapper opens an air door to allow a trammer and his tub of coal to pass through. Author's collection

(17) Pit: Warren Vale/Rawmarsh

Location: Rawmarsh, Rotherham
Type: Explosion
Fatalities: 23
Date: Friday 20 November 1874

In the wake of the Oaks a number of smaller incidents and accidents occurred at South Yorkshire pits. One of the worst was at Brightside, near Sheffield when five men were flung down the shaft, and killed, in a cage-winding accident. The cause was thought to have been due to a manufacturing fault in the rope that was being used. In 1870, one of two men killed in a roof fall at Agnes Main Colliery, Barnsley was described as 'one of the last survivors from the explosion at the Old Oaks Colliery in 1866'. An unusual occurrence was reported at Darfield Main two years later when 45 horses were killed in an underground fire. The immediate post-Oaks years, however, were notable for two disasters. The first occurred near Rotherham, at Warren Vale Colliery in 1874, resulting in twenty-three deaths. The second, a year later, was at Swaithe Main, when 143 men and boys died. In between these was the explosion at Aldwarke Main when seven deaths were recorded. Swaithe was the third worst South Yorkshire pit disaster and, fortunately, the last to involve more than a hundred fatalities.

Warren Vale entered the ranks of South Yorkshire collieries that had experienced more than one disaster when an explosion occurred in the dip levels of the Barnsley seam towards the end of 1874. Twenty-two years earlier, as we have already seen, fifty-two men lost their lives at the same pit.

Still under the control of the Charlesworths, there were 460 men and boys under-ground on the morning of 20 November when, at about 7.20, the fire-trier in the pit-bottom (Thomas Roebuck) heard someone say, 'Oh dear! Something is up.' The pit's engineer, George Johnson Kell, who had been employed there for twelve years, descended the shaft at 10.10 am and met Roebuck but there was no evidence of any fire. As a precaution, Kell issued an instruction to extinguish the pit furnace. Men were then found suffering from the effects of afterdamp.

A useful record of the disaster was provided by a local mining engineer, John Fretwell Thompson who came to Warren Vale in order to provide support. This was a common occurrence in the days when there was no properly organised system of rescue. Thompson lived nearby, at Wath and was employed at Manvers Main. The report also highlights the highly dangerous nature of such operations, reliant on experienced volunteers, equipped with minimal safety equipment. Thompson's account reads as follows:

> When I got to the pit I saw the manager, Mr Hargreaves and asked him if I could be of assistance. He asked me to go down the pit and I went down. In the engine plane I met Mr Kell and others just where the explosion had taken place. We went to examine the bottom of the gates in the first bank and found it full of gas. We then had a consultation and we decided to go and re-light the furnace. I took charge of the exploration party . . . When I got back to the level end, I took some men with me, and examined the stoppings, which had been put up in a great hurry and required repairing. We then got into the second gate in the far bank. I then ascertained how far the gas had got up there. When we got half way . . .

we found a body. We went a few yards further and found another two. We found gas on the far side of the bank next to the face. I then examined the levels coming round to the far gate again . . . There were two bodies in the first gate and a fire. We tried to put it out but did not succeed. All the men left the pit with the exception of Ward, Brown, Firth and Lazenby. We went to the fire . . . We got it out as best we could with the assistance of a bottle of water. There was a deal of smoke and there was gas five or six feet off. We found the body of xxxxxx and there was a stone on his head which had killed him. We then came across the bank face, the roof of which was heavily weighted. We found two [dead] men at the far side of the first bank, near the second gate. We found four near the far gate of the first bank. We came to the level and, after a short rest, went back and brought out one man out of the gate to the level and found that we could do no more. I sent out of the pit a note for fresh men and when they came we got the bodies out.

The inquest was conducted under the district coroner, Mr D Whiteman. The regional mines' inspector, Mr Wardell, was present, assisted by his colleague, Thomas Evans.

John Thompson thought that the cause of the explosion was a fall of roof in the goaf [old worked-out waste area] which 'drove out the gas'. Interestingly, and still fairly typical of the time, several colliers said that they still preferred to work with candles rather than with Stephenson lamps. The lamps, with their protected flames did not give as much light as the candles but had been introduced by the owners and the manager, William Hargreaves.

The predictable verdict of the jury was as follows:

Colliers continued to work with candles even when safety lamps were available. It is important to remember that they were invariably paid according to the coal that they extracted so a better light helped with this task. They must have been aware of the risks involved. Author's collection

That the deceased were accidentally killed by an explosion of gas at the Rawmarsh Colliery [Warren Vale] on the 20th, and that the jury recommend that Mr Wardell's recommendations [regarding the use of safety lamps] should be adhered to.

Some of those who died were as follows:

William Byron	Frederick Cliff
William Cooper	John Jowett
George King	James Mort
Isaac Oxley	Luke Oxley
Thomas Roberts	Samuel Skelton
Henry Stead	George Taylor
Samuel Thompson	John Tomlinson
Ben Turner	John Walker
John Woodin	George Wright

(18) Pit: Aldwarke Main

Location: Rotherham
Type: Explosion
Fatalities: 7
Date: 5 January 1875

A few weeks after Warren Vale, a neighbouring pit suffered a serious explosion and, yet again, blame was attributed to the use of candles instead of safety lamps.

Aldwarke Main, along with the nearby Carr House Colliery, had been purchased by the John Brown company of Sheffield in about 1873 and appears to have been worked as a single concern. The coal, from the Barnsley seam, came up from the Aldwarke pit. The upcast at Carr was used, at least in part, to support Aldwarke. One part of Aldwarke, known as the Third South Level had, prior to the Brown take-over, been worked by the proprietors of Carr House, so the two collieries were connected underground. A wall was built to support the roof at the junction between the two pits and a brattice placed there to facilitate ventilation.

The explosion took place in the South Level of the Carr House workings at about 6.20 am when there were 120 (a report in *The Times* states 312) men and boys underground. This location was about a mile from the Aldwarke shaft. A message was immediately sent to the pit top and signals began the process of winding all the miners to the surface – apart from seven or eight who could not be found.

Thomas Speight, the deputy on duty on the morning of the disaster, had earlier reported that the Carr House workings were 'all right and safe'. He was in the pit bottom and could not hear anything but this was over a thousand yards from the explosion. However, a young workman reported to him that his father had noticed gas in the South Level. Believing that the ventilation was 'good' there, Speight dispatched Holroyd, another deputy, to see if there was in fact any danger, and then followed. An explosion was clearly evident. On arrival, the body of a miner called Samuel Usherwood, a trammer from Rawmarsh, was found. His remains were, according to *The Times*, 'shockingly burned and disfigured'. It was then taken to the home of George Cooper who was also killed in the explosion.

The process of clearing the air in order to search for the bodies had been by no means straightforward, as explained in *The Times* of 6 January 1875:

So noxious was the gas that several persons in the exploring parties succumbed to its influence and had to be assisted up the shaft, one or two of them nearly unconscious. Repeated attempts were made to get into the workings, but the explorers were pressed back by the gas which it was impossible to penetrate. At last a novel expedient was resorted in order to clear the air in the workings. Fires were ignited in the Carr House Colliery . . . and a string of draught was caused, by which the noxious gases were drawn out of the South Level into the old workings and then the exploring party were able to enter.

Robert Copley, a fire-trier at the colliery, had been on duty the night before the explosion, fortuitously coming out of the pit at 6 am. He later stated that there was nothing to indicate any problems regarding the roadways or the ventilation in the south area. He further stated that gas had never been found in the mine before, other than in the old, deep workings. Copley was in bed when he was told about the explosion. He returned to the pit and went down to assist with the rescue operations but got overcome by the afterdamp.

A crowd of local people gathered on the pit bank as soon as news of the disaster spread. The first body was brought out 'amid the tears of anxious women and the cries of terrified children' according to the report in *The Times*. Some relatives waited for news for eight or nine hours, many still present 'when darkness fell, watching the ascent of the cage with terrible earnestness'. It was only after being informed that the recovery of bodies would take many more hours that the crowd dispersed, just leaving the pit officials and rescuers at the colliery.

The remaining dead miners were found beneath fallen material from the pack wall, blasted on top of them by the explosion.

The inquest was held under the coroner, Mr D Wightman who was very critical of a report by Mr Ford that had been placed before the jury following an impromptu inspection of the colliery. This unofficial account stated that no-one was to blame but the coroner said that it was improper to present such material to the jury before they had heard evidence on oath. Mr FN Wardell, the district inspector of mines was also in attendance.

The eventual outcome was the usual 'accidental death' verdict but the coroner made recommendations that the use of naked lamps should be discontinued in favour of safety lamps; and also that more deputies should be appointed. The jury also referred to lax record-keeping at the pit. The colliery manager, Mr Parker Rhodes, assured the jury that their recommendations would be implemented in full.

Those killed in the disaster were all young men, named as follows:

Richard Bennett, collier, 25, Rawmarsh, married
George Burkitt, trammer, Parkgate, left a widow and 3 children.
George Cooper, collier, 29, Rawmarsh Hill, left a widow and 3 children
Benjamin Elle (or Edge), 21, trammer, Parkgate, single
Thomas Griffiths, 35, collier, Maughan Quarry, married and 1 child
William Littlewood [or Whitehead], 24, trammer
Samuel Usherwood, 19, trammer, Rawmarsh Hill, single (brother-in-law of George
    Cooper)

(19) Pit: Swaithe Main

Location: Worsbrough Dale, Barnsley
Type: Explosion
Fatalities: 143
Date: Monday 6 December 1875

Set amid a most peaceful and picturesque of area, the explosion and huge death toll at Swaithe Main – making it one of the worst mining disasters in Britain – once more focussed media attention on Barnsley. Under the headline TERRIBLE COLLIERY ACCIDENTS, a report extending to almost two full columns appeared in the *Manchester Guardian*, the day after the disaster. Here are the opening few sentences:

> *About half-past nine o'clock yesterday morning the inhabitants of Swaithe and Worsbrough, about three miles from Barnsley, a large number of whom have relatives working at Swaithe and Edmunds Main Collieries, were startled by the report of an explosion at the former colliery. On running out of their houses they saw the bank of the pit enveloped in smoke, and a rush was at once made to the place. The scene was then, as usual in such cases, of the most agonising description.*

An updated account from Sheffield 'by telegraph' was added, containing details of the rescue operations, making the point that only two of the dead had been identified: George Blackburn, 55, Waltham Street, Barnsley and Thomas Markley, 24, Barley Street, also from Barnsley. Many of the bodies were said to have been so 'dreadfully mutilated' that immediate recognition was impossible, their clothes 'blown to shreds'. A 'later'

Swaithe Main colliery, as shown in the Illustrated London News, *18 December 1875.*
www.cmhrc.co.uk

report 'from our own correspondent' (in Barnsley), provided more details about the scene at the pit bank, including the arrival of Mr Wardle, the government's inspector of mines and a host of officials and engineers from neighbouring pits.

The *Guardian* also reported on the deaths of twelve miners in an explosion at Llan Colliery, near Cardiff and the inquest on the bodies of seven men killed in a shaft accident at the Alexandra pit in Wigan. But that was not the end of the story. The same page also contained brief accounts of the inquest on twenty-two miners who lost their lives in an explosion at Duffryn pit, Monmouthshire and reports about 'everyday' deaths at two local pits: one fatality at Agecroft Colliery and another at Cloughside.

In the new age of the telegraph, national coverage about Swaithe included *The Times* and, of course, the graphic pages of the *Illustrated London News*, as well as all the regional presses of Yorkshire.

Locally, and as one would expect, there was very detailed and extensive reportage in the columns of the *Barnsley Chronicle*, composed in typical Victorian style:

The pit has fired! Such was the brief but terribly significant announcement which was passed from mouth to mouth, with telegraphic rapidity in the little country hamlet of Swaithe on Monday morning last. What a depth of meaning was contained in these four monosyllables. So far, indeed, as residents in the immediate neighbourhood of the pit were concerned, words were unnecessary. It required no human tongue to tell the tale. No messengers however fleet of foot, no verbal announcement however epigrammatic, no telegraphist even how expert could have made the intimation so speedily and so effectually as it was made by one dread and unmistakable sound. A dull underground rumbling, the sound of distant thunder, followed by a heavy boom, fell like a death knell upon the inmates of many miners' cottages and resulted in an instant rush to the road of frantic wives and weeping children. By many at a distance the news was conveyed to the eye before it reached the ear. A rush from the pit shaft of smoke and dust which for a moment completely enveloped the headgear and hung like a pall over the pit hill and its surroundings was a signal not to be mistaken by anyone who has had previous experience of colliery disasters.

Swaithe was the sister pit of Edmunds Main, both concerns the property of partners J Mitchell (of Swaithe Hall or House), C Bartholomew (Doncaster) and J Tyas (Barnsley). The pits were about a mile apart. Swaithe opened in 1860 and, from 1863, an inclined plane connected it to Edmunds Main. The Swaithe explosion occurred almost thirteen years to the day following the Edmunds disaster of 1862. Thus the company and local communities were badly affected by two major disasters in a relatively short period.

Swaithe's downcast shaft (used for drawing) was 13 ft. 6 inches in diameter and sunk to 320 yards. The upcast was slightly smaller, at 12ft 9 inches and reached 230 yards where there was a ventilating furnace. The upcast was unmistakable at the surface because of its iron chimney. A distance of 68 yards separated the two shafts. The sturdy headgear of pitch-pine was 56 ft high, supporting a pair of 17 ft pulleys operated via two 60 hp steam winding engines.

The coal worked was from the notoriously fiery Barnsley Nine Foot bed but the pit was not regarded as being dangerous, and locked safety lamps were in compulsory use. Production was good, some 7,800 tons a week, mostly sent to the lucrative London and southern markets.

It was fortunate that the disaster took place on 'Saint Monday', the traditional day that miners 'laiked' or rested from work, or the fatalities would have been significantly greater. Some men had swapped shifts with friends in order to watch a greyhound race at the nearby Dillington Stadium. Afterwards their emotions must have been very mixed: a feeling of responsibility for their obliging mates who got injured or killed and a great sense of relief at their own lucky 'escape'.

The explosion occurred at 9.40 am when there were about 240 men and boys underground. Most, about 200, worked in the South Level, in a dip towards the Edmunds Main shaft. The other men were in the northern workings. A 'loud report' was easily heard by men at the pit bank, followed by the usual rush of gas and smoke up the shafts.

Among the early arrivals were John Mitchell, the certified pit manager and his brother, Joseph Mitchell jnr , together with a large group of neighbouring managers and engineers. The government inspector for the district, F N Wardell was also in attendance as were several local doctors and surgeons. A rescue operation was soon in place, led by John Mitchell. The descent was successful until a blockage was encountered almost at the bottom, so ladders had to be used. Wedged in the sump was local man, George Linford, still alive, so he was promptly placed in the cage and sent to the surface. Men who had managed to reach the pit bottom from the workings were in a very bad condition, delirious because of the gas. During the day sixteen men and boys were brought out alive and there was great relief when information came through that seventy to eighty men had escaped via the Edmunds Main shaft. At the time it was feared that 120 men had been lost, a figure which was soon to increase to more than 140.

It soon became clear that the blast had originated in the lower dip where most of the men were working. Walking a distance of about fifty yards, the bodies of a man and boy

Recovery of the dead at Swaithe Main following the explosion, as shown in the Illustrated London News. www.cmhrc.co.uk

were found, apparently overtaken in their attempt to escape by the afterdamp. More dead bodies were found as the exploration continued in the direct of the southern workings. By 1 pm a fire was discovered, delaying matters until the flames were extinguished. There were more than enough volunteers to assist with the rescue operations. One brave chap, William Midgely, succeeded in rescuing three more men, each found in an exhausted condition. By 2 pm the ventilation system was working again, enabling further explorations to take place. Once again, miners found dead in their working places were passed over in the hope of reaching some sign of life. After several hours of searching, the grim task of recovering bodies was the only option.

On Tuesday, the day after the explosion, the exploring parties had succeeded in getting out thirty-four bodies, only one of them alive but he died within an hour of reaching the surface. More bodies were brought out on Wednesday, the death toll rising to 110 by the afternoon.

The colliery's joiners' shop and saw mill were converted into a temporary hospital and morgue. Those found alive and treated were conveyed to Barnsley's Beckett Hospital. A graphic description of the 'dead house' was given in the *Barnsley Chronicle*:

The sight was truly a ghastly one over which few would desire to linger. There were those whose features were as composed as if death had overtaken them whilst placidly at sleep. Whilst . . . [others had] features . . . distorted by terror, their glassy eyeballs staring from their sockets and their hands clasped in agony. In some cases every bone in the body was broken, whilst others it was the head and upper part of the body which had suffered. One poor lad had his head entirely blown away. In another case half the skull had been blown away . . . The faces had been washed in order that identification might be rendered more easy . . . In many cases identification, even by wives and sons was almost, if not altogether impossible . . . In one case a body was identified as that of John Wadsworth with the intention of being forwarded to Wadsworth's residence. During the afternoon, however, Mr Charles Lees of Barnsley arrived, and found that the body was that of John Waterworth of Swaithe, not Wadsworth of Barnsley. We note that each body was distinguished by a number, that which was first brought out being No.1; the second No.2, and so on. The police officer . . . took possession of the property of the deceased, rolled it in paper, and marked it with a number corresponding to that of the body.

Soon, the saw mill was full of bodies, so the colliery's pay office was used. This, too, got full, and a cart shed adapted; yet again this filled with bodies, so a store room was emptied and adapted, the bodies laid in rows. The waiting crowd formed an avenue through which corpses were carried. Thirty surplus and unused coffins from the 1866 Oaks disaster were used once bodies had been identified. Only six of the forty-five horses in the pit survived, their carcases described as having 'all the hair burnt from their bodies, which were of a reddish-brown colour'. Some horses were so badly swollen that they would not fit into the cage, so had to be cut into pieces.

Survivors were interviewed by the press. George Beardsall, one of the pit deputies, spoke to the *Sheffield Telegraph*:

The first I knew of the explosion was by seeing men running to the shaft at the Edmunds Main end. I could have got out . . . but I stopped behind to help others . . . I tried my best to get to the Swaithe Main side but stopped in too long and the afterdamp came upon me. I saw a lot of men go to the shaft and get out . . . I liberated nine of them . . . I then went down as far as I could to get the other way, and passed the bodies of three colliers. They were lying about 150 yards from the Swaithe Main shaft. I recognised two of them, they were Henry Daley, a miner, and John Waterworth, a deputy. I could proceed no further owing to the afterdamp . . . Two men held my arms and took me to the Edmunds Main shaft . . . [and brought me out].

James White, who lived at Stairfoot, was working with his trammer, Thomas Leary when the latter noticed a change of air and 'a strong sulphurous smell'. White started paying but, seeing his trammer running away decided to follow. From their working place in Edmunds Jenny they ran down the main level where they met a man from the bottom of the shaft whose light had been blown out. The afterdamp continued so the three of them continued running until reaching one roadway which was reduced to only 2 ft high, the roof having caved in, so crawled as fast as they could, eventually escaping via the Edmunds shaft.

The adjourned inquest was held at Barnsley Court House on Thursday 16 December before coroner T Taylor. Miners who had been members of the South Yorkshire Miners' Association were represented by Mr Hopwood, QC, MP. John Mitchell, the colliery manager had his own representative, Mr John Miller, QC and Mr Shaw spoke on behalf of the colliery company. The deputies and underviewers had their own solicitor in attendance, Mr Parker Rhodes of Rotherham. Two government inspectors of mines were present: Mr Wardell (South Yorkshire) and Mr Evans (Derbyshire).

Swaithe deputy Joseph Bennett who was on the day shift on the fateful day of the explosion was questioned. Bennett, who had gone down the pit at 5.25 am, explained how he had met fellow day deputy, Henry Jacques, in the box-hole. Two night deputies – Joseph Sheldon and William Midgely – were at the bottom of the shaft, checking the lamps of the miners when they had descended. Both men were subsequently killed. Sheldon had written a note to indicate that all was in order. Bennett went to Brigg's Siding because gas had been noticed there. It had been present for about three weeks and repeatedly reported up to two days before the explosion. A shot was fired in Joshua Eyre's working place, in No. 3 district, fired by a fuse lit by a wire made red hot in Earnshaw's lamp. Coal came down in the usual way and Eyre began filling the fallen debris. After assisting two men to free a rope which had got trapped under a sleeper, all three men experienced 'a tremendous rush of air up the double three jenny'. Progress was hindered because of the afterdamp but, crawling, he reached Brigg's siding and, with others, escaped through the Edmunds Main shaft. Other evidence showed that the explosion did not take place until 45 minutes after the shot had been fired.

Another interviewee was labourer John Godfrey of Copper Street, Barnsley. Like Bennett, he went down the mine between five and six on the morning of the 6th. At 10 am a wind blew out his light, so he made his way to the pit bottom but the main roadway or engine plane was full of afterdamp so had to retrace his steps, getting to the bottom by means of 'a back travelling road'.

Another witness, Robert Schofield, a collier who worked regular 'afternoons' said that he was in the pit on the Saturday before the explosion and he did not notice any problems with the ventilation. On the previous Monday he was given a two-pound canister full of gunpowder by a man called Bostock. After the explosion Schofield assisted with the rescue operations.

Swaithe deputy William Midgely had been on duty up to 6 am on the morning of the explosion and everything 'was of good order'. Later, on the Tuesday, he assisted with the rescue operations, finding John Nettleship still alive.

Mining engineer Robert Miller of Stratford Main informed the jury that the explosion may have been a consequence of gas being driven through the gauze of a saftey lamp following a fall of coal after blasting. He recommended the use of Stephenson rather than Davy lamps and questioned the practice of blasting in the Barnsley and Silkstone beds.

After a lengthy summing up by the coroner and two hour deliberation by the jury the following verdict was announced:

> *The jury find that Thomas Blackburn, James Allen and others came to their deaths at the Swaithe Main Colliery by an explosion or explosions of firedamp but how such explosion or explosions originated there is not sufficient evidence to show. We are likewise of the opinion that, according to the evidence the Swaithe Main Colliery a fiery mine and that the General and Special Rules have not been rigidly carried out and that gunpowder has been recklessly used. The jury are also of the opinion that in all mines where safety lamps are used the use of gunpowder should not be allowed except in the stone drifts, and there only when the miners are drawn out. The jury desire the coroner to forward this opinion to the Secretary of State. We also regret that the miners have not carried out General Rule 30, and think that this rule should be strictly adhered to.*

Although the exact cause of the Swaithe disaster was never conclusively identified, new scientific research began to demonstrate the significance of coal dust in many explosions in British coal mines.

The fatality list (below) shows that most of the miners were young family men aged between 20–40. There was only one miner, Henry Grant, over the age of 50, emphasising the highly physical nature of the job. It is interesting to see that there were a few immigrant, Polish, miners employed. The list includes ten children aged 12–14. Children as young as twelve continued to be employed in mining until the Coal Mines Act of 1911. As we would expect, most of the workforce lived near to the pit, from the hamlet of Swaithe itself, Worsbrough Dale and Worsbrough Bridge, though a few walked (there and back!) at least ten miles a day.

Worsbrough Dale

Henry William Bailey, 20	William Bamforth, 20
Gad Bardon, 43, married, 5 children	Benjamin Bennett, 29, married, 3 children
Pharaoh Bostock, 14	Alfred Bower, 14
Edward Bower, 12	Isaac Bullock, 29
Thomas Bullock, 30	Edward George Carr, 24, married, 1 child
Thomas Coxon, 18	Thomas Carrersal, 24, married
Joshua Eyre, 22, married, 1 child	William Earnshaw, 32, married, 3 children
John Gibson, 14	Alfred Gilbert, 21, married, 3 children
Edwin Glover, 19	William Greenbank, 27, married
George Halmshaw, 14	Albert Harrison, 14
Jura Herod (Polish), 29, married, 1 child	Alfred Hoyland, 29
	William Hudson, 30, married
Paul Kendal, 49, married, 6 children	Paul Kendal, 15
William George Kendal, 17	Thomas Kilburn, 29, married, 1 child

Fred Kilner, 14
       3 children
Thomas Lancashire, 24, married
Thomas Maltby, 24, married, 1 child
Joseph Morton, 20
Arthur Netherwood, 18
John Edward Philips, 18
Amos Semley, 14
Richard Smith, 29, married, 3 children
William Smith, 30, married, 8 children
Thomas Watson, 16
Joseph Watson, 18
Joseph Winder Pashley, 21

Andreas Konnuck (Polish), 33, married,
Israel Lambert, 19
William Laughton, 17
Charles Morton, 20
Joseph Noble, 38, married, 3 children
John Nicholson, 17
Edward Semley, 17
George Slater, 20
John Thomas Smith, 17
John Stowroski (Polish), 44, married,
      4 children
Robert Wilkinson, 20
Thomas Woodhead, 29

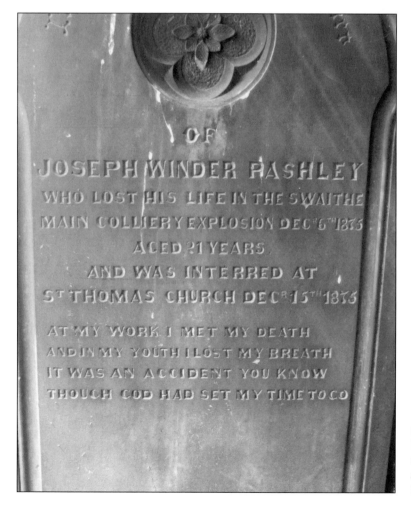

Gravestone of Joseph Winder Pashley who died in the Swaithe disaster of 1875. Photo: Brian Elliott

Worsbrough Common

George Armitage, 52, married,
    5 children
Henry Bell, 16
Charles Henry Collumbine, 16
James Green, 43
John Heppinstall, 46, married, 1 child
Thomas Lockwood, 16
Joseph Mowbery Robinson, 19
William Walter, 16
George Wildsmith, 19

James Barrowclough, 30, married,
    4 children
Henry Cawthorn, 22
Leonard Galloway, 16
Joseph Harrison, 19, married
Thomas Lockwood, 50, married, 4 children
James McCullough, 17
William Charles Tyas, 20
John Waller, 14

Gravestone of John Pickering, killed at Swaithe Main in the 1875 disaster. Photo: Brian Elliott

Barnsley

Frank Allen, 18
Henry Ackers, 25, married, 2 children
William Bray, 24, married, 2 children
William Buckley, 33, married, 1 child
William Carr, 40, married, 5 children
J Dolan, 29, married, 3 children
George Evans, 17
Thomas Lund, 24
Thomas Markey, 25, married
Robert McNaught, 40
William Oates, 45, married, 5 children
John Pickering, 23, married, 1 child
A Rock, 23
J Sedgewick, 31, married, 4 children
James Temperley, 34, married,
    5 children

William Allen, 19
James Blackburn, 45, married
John Brown, 36, married, 5 children
J Calvert, married, 2 childen
Alfred Crackles, 24, married, 2 children
Arthur Dunk, 20, married, 1 child
William Goodliff, 22, married
Henry Malin, 22, married
Henry Marsden, 25, married, 1 child
James Muldoon, 31, married, 3 children
George Philipson, 30
T Rider, 16
Edward Rose, 23
Henry Stott, 17
Walter Whitham, 19, unmarried
John Wood, 19

Swaithe

James Allen, 32, married, 4 children
Thomas Beevors, 47, married, 1 child
James Denton, 32, married
John Goodall, 48, married
Charles Harrison, 13
Thomas Scorah, 31, married, 1 child
Joseph Sheldon, 43, married, 3 children
Henry Charles Vine, 20
Blacker Hill
George Fawcett, 29, married, 4 children
Edward Jenkins, 21
Fred J Moore, 26, married, 3 children

George Banks, 38, married, 9 children
George Beresford, 53
John Gilbert, 20, married, 1 child
Charles Goodman, 19
Henry Jacques, 27, married, 2 children
John Semley, 17
George Sykes, 25, married, 2 children
John Waterworth, 30, married, 5 children
Joseph Dodson, 32, married, 2 children
J Tranter, 23
William Jenkins, 25, married, 2 children

Stairfoot

J Benson, 14
A James Hancock, 34, married,
    4 children
William Walker, 29, married
John Christian, 32, married
J Partlett, 19, married, 1 child

William Brown, 19
John Jenkins, 26, married, 2 children
Samuel Schofield, 35, married, 4 children
Mesborough Dyke
Thomas Foster, 29, married, 2 children

Wombwell

William Nettleship, 23, married,
    2 children

William Rodgers, 32, married, 1 child
Fred Holt Waldie, 21, married, 1 child

Platts Common

Samuel Green, 27, married, 4 children
Charles Taylor, 26, married, 3 children

Charles Hall, 24

The memorial to the Swaithe Main disaster can be seen in the churchyard of St Thomas's church, Worsbrough Dale.
Photos: Brian Elliott

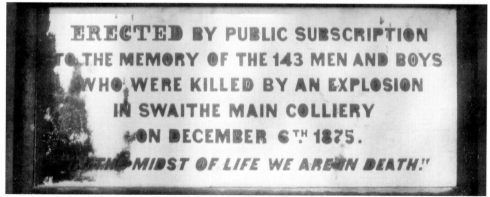

ERECTED BY PUBLIC SUBSCRIPTION TO THE MEMORY OF THE 143 MEN AND BOYS WHO WERE KILLED BY AN EXPLOSION IN SWAITHE MAIN COLLIERY ON DECEMBER 6TH 1875. "IN THE MIDST OF LIFE WE ARE IN DEATH."

Nether Hoyland
John Bailey, 25, married, 2 children   Samuel Hague, 35, married, 2 children

Cliff Bridge
William Tyas, 43, married, 6 children

Hoyle Mill
Henry Grant, 55, married, 6 children

Jump
Levi Henry Thickett, 18

Darfield
Thomas William Senior, 17

As at the Oaks nine years earlier, a variety of objects were produced to commemorate the Swaithe disaster, most notably a pair of plates. A public subscription financed a distinctive memorial, placed outside St Thomas's church, Worsbrough Dale in 1878. Individual gravestones to disaster victims are extant in several local churchyards and Barnsley cemetery.

The situation of raising sufficient funds in support of deceaseds' widows and children of disaster victims continued to result in understandable criticism from many quarters. The Swaithe Main Colliery Fund was established within the somewhat awkward context of a large surplus being still available in the Oaks fund; and yet dependants of the latter, as has already been noted, received minimal financial support. Many people, especially the miners themselves, felt that the colliery owners should be the main provider of relief. There were seventy-two widows and 168 children needing urgent assistance. The Swaithe partners disagreed with each other over the amount of money that the company should give to the fund, eventually providing £1,000, though there was a separate and substantial personal donation of £3,000 from Mr John Tyas, one of the partners. As usual, there was support from the Mayor of London's Mansion House Fund, a deputation securing at least £2,500. The total of subscriptions was expected to reach £10,000. Furthermore, the benefit funds of the South Yorkshire Miners' Association were inadequate and unreliable sources of assistance at this time.

The inadequacies of both the public subscriptions and union as the main sources of relief led, after a series of meeting, to the more efficient establishment of the West Riding of Yorkshire Permanent Relief Fund in March 1877. By the end of the year it had almost 4,000 members in thirty-nine branches throughout Yorkshire and north Derbyshire. This well-organised body – unlike its ad hoc predecessors – did deliver benefits 'as promised'. Many colliery companies deducted subscriptions at source, reducing the chances of a miner forgetting to keep his membership up to date. By the time of the Wharncliffe Carlton disaster of 1883 (see below) the WRYPRF had over 16,000 members (about 1 in 4 of all mineworkers), a considerable achievement. It had become the dominant provider of relief and assistance to those injured and bereaved in mining accidents and disasters. Thus, the Swaithe disaster was a major factor in the establishment of the first proper and efficient organisation to assist the families of Yorkshire miners during and after periods of sudden distress.

This trophy was presented to Joseph Mitchell for his 'valuable services' in the Swaithe disaster of 1875 from the Edmunds and Swaithe Coal Company. Author's collection.

Swaithe, along with its sister pit, Edmunds Main, continued to function, though one of the chief partners, Joseph Mitchell – said to be badly affected by the disaster – died in January 1876. The end for Swaithe Main came in 1894, the Barnsley Bed having been exhausted and the thinner beds offering little promise. The old coke ovens, however, remained in operation until 1908. Over a generation or so, these ill-fated collieries had provided a place of work for hundreds of men and boys as well as profits for the owners – but at a tremendous human cost.

After Swaithe accidents and disasters on the South Yorkshire coalfield became less frequent. However, even though there were no fatalities, both the Old and New Oaks collieries experienced several sudden and serious discharges of gas during 1876–77. Two new pits, Mitchell Main and Cortonwood, also suffered similar gas outbursts between 1877–78; and Barrow Colliery had an underground fire in 1882. Towards the end of November of the same year four men were killed in an explosion at Kiveton Park Colliery. The last major explosion of firedamp in a troubled century of disasters took place at Wharncliffe Carlton pit in 1883, when 20 men were killed.

(20) Pit: Wharncliffe Carlton

Location: Smithies, Barnsley
Type: Explosion
Fatalities: 20
Date: Thursday 18 October 1883

Several collieries were established in the Smithies area of Barnsley, off Wakefield Road, during the second half of the nineteenth century. One of the most notable was Robert Craik's pit on the New Lodge estate (soon to be known as East Gawber Hall Colliery), sunk in 1854 by Jaggers. A Scotsman, Craik rose from modest beginnings as an apprentice draper in Barnsley to become one of the town's leading linen entrepreneurs and public figures. His new mining concern was operational by 1858, the coal traded initially highly dependant on transport by canal. Craik's employees increased from 260 in 1864 to about 800 in 1883, reflecting growing business activity. Yet safety did not seem to be too great a concern. In 1861 Charles Morton, the district inspector of mines, reported that, contrary to his advice in the wake of the Lundhill catastrophe, and 'for the sake of cheapness', the use of safety lamps 'was unwisely abandoned' at East Gawber. The Barnsley bed of coal caught fire and the colliery's underground viewer (Mark Ward) and his deputy (John Warhurst) lost their lives following an explosion.

In 1872 the Craik family had a new shaft sunk adjacent to the recently opened Barnsley Coal Railway, about half a mile from their main colliery, and named Wharncliffe Carlton. The two pits were connected underground. The new enterprise was 130 yards deep and worked by the longwall system. Stephenson and Clanny lamps were reported to have been in use. The owners used the services of the well-known local mining engineer Joseph Mitchell on a consultative basis. John Slack had managed both collieries for fifteen months. The under-manager was Herbert Fisher. The deputies were said to have 'understood their duties' apart from George Micklethwaite who – in a special report – was criticised by the Yorkshire MP Arnold Morley as not being 'a fit person to hold a responsible position in a colliery'.

The disaster at Wharncliffe Carlton was bad enough, involving twenty deaths, but

Wharncliffe Carlton Colliery at the time of the 1883 disaster, as published in the Illustrated London News. Author's collection

could have been far more serious if the explosion had taken place during the day when the usual complement of 176 men and boys would have been underground. In the event there were only twenty-five maintenance men down the pit, on the night-shift, when the explosion occurred, at about midnight. Only five of these escaped with their lives.

News of the Wharncliffe Carlton disaster did not escape the attention of the national press. The following extract, taken from *The Times* of 20 October 1883, captures the drama of the occasion:

> *At ten o'clock on Thursday night 25 men were lowered into the pit. Two hours later a loud report was heard, compared by some who heard it to the sound of a cannon. A cloud of smoke was then seen to rush from the pit high up in the air, and then all was still. Mr. John Slack, the manager, and Mr Herbert Fisher, the under manager, were soon on the pit bank proffering assistance. Before their arrival a faint voice was heard calling for help. The engine man tried to raise the cage but found it impossible. Those below were told of this, and they set to work to clear away the masses of dirt and rubbish which had been blown from the workings to the pit bottom, and which weighed the cage so that it could not be moved. On this being done [debris cleared], it was found that the cage could be moved . . . Five men who had been working near the pit bottom were then brought out alive. These were W. Clement, J. Glover, D. Scattergood, E. Moore, and H. Westwood. The only one who was hurt was clover, horse-keeper, whose face was cut by a piece of dirt which had blown against it. A band of explorers, conducted by Mr. Slack and Mr. Fisher, descended the pit at 2 am. They found the roads blocked by a large fall of roof, brought about by the*

violence of the explosion. The air courses were stopped up, and it was impossible to get far . . . till the obstructions were cleared away. Sixty volunteers working in shifts set to do this dangerous work. The afterdamp was so powerful that volunteer after volunteer fainted away, and had to be brought out . . . thoroughly exhausted. They succeeded . . . in getting along the main plane some 1,200 yards, where three dead bodies were found.

The report continued:

The first dead body removed was that of William Fisher of Commercial Street, Barnsley; William Lawson, of Wood Street, Barnsley, was the next man found; and John Wright, of Grace Street, Barnsley was found fifteen minutes later. As these were brought to the surface they were examined by Dr Blackburn, Mr Foster, his assistance, and Mr Halton, surgeon, who found them quite dead. Their features were calm and placid, and it seems evident that they had been suffocated by the afterdamp, two of them found having their hands raised to their faces as though to protect them. The doctors noticed, too, that while the bodies were burnt about the hands, and were slightly singed, there was none of those severe burns which had been found on the victims of previous explosions in the Barnsley seam. In the hope that others might be near, the explorers laboured bravely on, but heavy falls in the main plane impeded their work. Mr. Joseph Mitchell, the consulting engineer, and Mr F.W. Wardell, the inspector for the district, considering it hopeless that any of the men left in the mine could possibly survive, thought it advisable not to risk the lives of explorers in the workings till further steps had been taken to restore ventilation. Both gentlemen were early down the pit, and remained there superintending arrangements for the restoration of ventilation . . .

The report concluded with:

The cause of the explosion is at present shrouded in mystery. It is believed to have taken place in deep workings, 1,700 yards from the pit bottom. A sad feature . . . is that there is no survivor left to give any narrative of what happened . . .

At the time that the inquest was convened three bodies had still not been recovered from the mine. The pit had had to be flooded in order to extinguish underground fires, therefore delaying any further explorations of the workings. The district coronor, Thomas Taylor took charge of the proceedings. Arnold Upton, one of the few survivors from the ill-fated night shift, described how the blast from the explosion knocked him down, causing the loss of his lamp which he abandoned as he felt that it was far too dangerous for him to search and retrieve. The survivors, with only three lamps between them, had great difficulty in avoiding roof falls and other obstacles in their slow progress towards safety. At the pit bottom it was realised that one man was missing so Lupton and another collier retreated to try to locate him. They found the missing individual, along with another miner. Both 'had not lost hope'.

At the time of the explosion the horse-keeper was struck down but not seriously injured. None of the pit's horses were killed.

The source of the explosion came from the 'dip' workings, the rush of air issuing from that direction, along the Engine Plane (main roadway). A theory put forward by the men was that the explosion occurred in the Engine Plane, following the firing of a shot near the Stone Drift. A shot-firer, William Fisher had taken cartridges down the pit, ready for blasting. His lamp was found near his body at the foot of the Stone Drift but there was no evidence of firing.

The following verdict was announced by the chairman of the jury:

That William Fisher and sixteen others were killed by an explosion of gas on the night of the 18th October in the Wharncliffe Carlton Colliery but how the explosion was caused there is no evidence to show.

Arnold Morley MP stated that there were no grounds 'for believing that the catastrophe was in any way due to bad management or misconduct of any person', so any legal action was ruled out.

Craik's collieries at Smithies continued to function through to the early 1890s when financial problems began to emerge. An unusual situation arose following an advertised sale of the collieries. The event was aborted due to a great protest by local colliers who – armed with pick shafts – chased the bailiffs away. Later, John Edey, a chartered accountant from Sheffield, obtained the lease of Craik's collieries but the coal extraction part of the venture did not last long, workings at Wharncliffe Carlton becoming exhausted or uneconomic by 1901. Coal production ceased during and shortly after the Great War.

A very useful essay by John Goodchild, relating to the numerous pits sited in the Smithies area and entitled 'Up Wakefield Road' can be seen in *Aspects of Barnsley 4* (Wharncliffe Books, 1998).

The men and boys who lost their lives were:

Ellis Ambler, 58, married, 2 children, Grace Street, Barnsley
Albert Button, 32, deputy, married, St Mark's Terrace, Wakefield Rd
George Egley, 55, married, no family, Honeywell Street
Henry Fisher, 'Uncle Harry', 54, married, 3 children, Middlesex Street
William Fisher, 41
James Flatney, aged 14
Richard Garbutt, 49, widower, 'with family', Mapplewell
William Goulding, 40, married, 4 children, John Street
John Hallam, 41, married, 2 children, John Street
Frederick Hollins [Holland?], alias 'Dot', 25, hurrier
William Lawson, 49, married, Wood Street
William Mason, 40, married, Bridge Street, Hoyle Mill
George Mason, 16, only son of above
Graham [Charles?] Philips, 54 [?], married, 6 children, Honeywell Street
George Philips, 19, hurrier, son of the above
William Shaw, 54, married, 6 children
Charles Starkey (East Gawber Hall Colliery), 36
Thomas Wood, 55, hurrier
Edward Willar [Weller], 28, hurrier, Park Row, Barnsley
John Wright, 46, married, 7 children, Tune Street

Fortunately, most if not all of the adult males were members of the West Riding Miners' Permanent Relief Fund, so widows and dependants did receive some financial assistance.

It is noticeable that this list contains a higher proportion of mature men than hitherto, though this probably reflects the demands of the night shift and the maintenance situation. However, many of us with mining ancestry will know that there were, before 1947, many miners working up to and beyond the age of seventy years.

(21) Pit: Houghton Main

Location: Darfield, Barnsley
Type: Winding accident
Fatalities: 10
Date: Thursday 30 December 1886

This terrible pit-cage accident was the last Victorian disaster to affect the area we now call South Yorkshire. All serious accidents and disasters, no matter what scale, are of course very upsetting for all those individuals closely associated with the men and boys killed or injured. The Houghton Main disaster, however, was a particularly sad one since seven of the ten victims belonged to just three families. It was also unusual in that the engineman, Allen Beresford, was indicted for manslaughter.

In 1886 Houghton Main was a new pit, operational for about eight years and, for the time, had a relatively good safety record, with only five fatalities recorded previously. It was one of the larger, new generation of collieries, employing about 690 men and boys.

At about 7.50 pm, at the end of the afternoon shift, ten men were being drawn up the shaft, occupying, as was normal practice, only the top platform of a three-deck cage. The draw for the men was always deliberately slower than when corves of coal were wound, taking three to four minutes. Allen Beresford, the pit's experienced engine winder,

employed there since the pit had opened, was generally regarded as a responsible and cool-headed man. When the cage was about 150 yards from the surface Beresford, sat in his chair, heard a cracking noise above him. This was all that he recalled of the disaster as he was struck on the forehead by a piece of wood and made, temporarily, unconscious. The worst situation imaginable had happened. The great cage had failed to hold at the surface, was overwound and smashed into the head-gear and roof of the engine house. The rope, made of the best steel, and over five inches in diameter, had a working strain of 110 tons. It was secured to the cage by means of a massive wrought-iron cappel, but the rope snapped and the cage hurtled back down the shaft with its terrified occupants, at terrific speed

A three-deck pit cage. This early example, one of the largest in Britain, was used at Silverwood colliery, near Rotherham. Author's collection

*Signalling an ascent.
The boys at the front of
the cage can hardly
reach the safety bar.*
Author's collection

over a distance of 535 yards. It has been estimated that if the cage weighed between 4 and 5 tons the descent would have taken no more than 12 seconds, and reached over 200 mph when it hit the bottom. On impact, it smashed through the massive oak beams over the sump 'as though they had been matchwood'. The car or cage was made of iron.

A report in *The Times* describes the scene of destruction at the pit top:

> . . . the gates which protected the shaft at the right-hand side were missing, as well as the rope which draws the cage. The cage had been carried away and one portion caught in the ironwork, fully 12 ft above the landing stage, and a portion which had formed the wood-work of the gates had been driven into the headgear. The floor was strewn with shattered pieces of wood [it was one of these that hit the engine man] which had been torn from the roof, while larger pieces had struck near the drum, round which the rope had been drawing the miners out of the pit.

A 'butterfly' or King's patent over-winding safety device was installed. The rope was supposed to detach from the cage into a catchplate or bell, enabling the cage to be suspended in mid-air. But the upward speed of the cage was so great that the device was smashed into fragments.

Below ground the prospect of anyone surving this horrendous fall was nil. It was thought that some of the miners may have died of shock at the point when the cage crashed into the headgear. No-one will ever know but the carnage in and around the pit bottom is too gruesome to describe in full. Suffice to say that the bodies were torn to pieces. Portions of clothing and footwear were found but most of the human remains lay in water, at the bottom of the sump.

The pit's manager, Mr J Scott Elliott and other officials attended the scene quickly but all they could do was to draw up, by means of the upcast shaft, the remaining men – over 100 of them – still in the mine. The upcast, designed for use in such emergencies, was about forty yards away. As was the legal requirement, a message was sent to the district inspector of mines, F N Wardell, informing him of the disaster; and also to the colliery engineer, Mr Jarratt who lived at Monk Bretton.

Beresford must have been in a distraught state when he fully realised what had happened. Three years earlier he was something of a hero when he averted what would have been a serious incident when a portion of flange of the pulley broke off when the men were being drawn up. He immediately stopped the engine and made good the damage.

Early visitors to the disaster scene were two senior police officers, Superintendent Kane and Inspector Gunn. After an investigation they ordered the arrest of Allen Beresford who was then taken into custody by PC Holmes. It was found that the indicator attached to the winding engine showed that the drum had made seven revolutions more than was needed to land the cage at the pit bank.

Engineers and officials at the top of the ill-fated shaft assembled on the Saturday and concentrated on the formidable task of raising the broken cage. This had to be accomplished before bodies in the sump could be accessed. The sump water could not be drained away because of the amount of human remains it contained. It was therefore decided to empty the sump by filling barrels with the water and then draw these grim containers up the shaft, a process that continued through the night and early the following morning. Once this had been completed the shattered bodies were placed in coffins which had been conveyed to the pit bottom by the colliery company. The bodies of Joseph Walker and his two sons were immediately recognised as were several others. But some bodies were 'in fragments' and totally unrecognisable.

The 'sad scenes' at the pit bank were described by a Barnsley news reporter:

Anxious crowds of relatives and friends, mingled with spectators, have been in the vicinity of the pit all day and many sad scenes have been witnessed. Some of the relations are wishful to have the bodies removed to their homes, and a special messenger was despatched to Barnsley during the day to lay the matter before Superintendent Kane. It has, however, been deemed best to allow the widows and relatives of the unfortunate men to carry out their own desires. The colliery company, who have made known their intention to defray all expenses of removal and interment are anxious to do all they can to soften the blow which has so suddenly fallen on the bereaved.

The inquest opened at the Cross Keys Inn, Darfield, before the district coroner, Mr Dossey Wightman. Those in attendance included F N Wardell, Her Majesty's Inspector of Mines and Mr W Parrott who represented the Miners' Association. Mr Wightman explained that the identification of the bodies was via evidence only. Certificates of burial could be issued as the relatives wanted the funerals to take place in the afternoon.

George Walker of Billingley, who was a miner at Houghton Main, confirmed the identification of his father, Joseph and his two brothers, Samuel and Charles. Another Houghton miner, Charles Hardcastle, identified the body of his father, James. A Darfield miner, James Wright (and other witnesses), gave evidence of identification in respect of his father-in-law, Joseph Pearson. Edward Baxter was identified by his brother, William. John Mannion identified his brother, William and Edmund Barton gave evidence of the identification of his brother, William. The inquest was then adjourned.

At the adjourned inquest evidence was heard from Charles Atkinson, hanger-on at the pit bottom, who narrowly escaped death when the cage smashed into the sump. He stated that he heard it coming down at great speed and got out of the way but saw the cage crash through the sump boards. Another key witness, Albert Holdsworth, who was banksman, and on duty at the time said that the usual signals were received and returned. As the cage neared the surface he heard a crash and the engine house was damaged. The lever at the pit bank could not be placed in position fast enough. However, it was thought that even if in position it would not have made any difference to the cage falling down the shaft. Holdsworth saw the engine man, Beresford, coming out of the building, saying that he had been hit by a piece of wood.

After a four hour deliberation the jury's verdict included the following:

The men had been killed by falling down the shaft when they had been overwound by Beresford.

Allen Beresford was charged with manslaughter and bound over for two weeks on bail.

The ten persons who were killed in the disaster were buried, together, in Darfield churchyard. A large crowd attended the ceremony, some travelling a good distance. Reverend H P Cooke, rector of Darfield and the Reverend F Sleep, vicar, performed the Church of England burial service for nine of the victims. William Mannion, a Roman Catholic, received a separate service, conducted by the Reverend H J Smith of St Helen's, Elsecar.

A granite monument inscribed with the names of the Houghton Main victims was erected on the grave site, in the south-west corner of the old churchyard, and unveiled in a commemorative ceremony on 12 November 1887 by the Houghton Main manager, J S Elliott.

The Beresford trial – at Leeds Assizes – attracted a great deal of public interest and press coverage.

Mr Harvey, representing the Treasury, outlined the circumstances of the accident. Charles Atkinson was again called to give evidence and there was testimony from Phillip White, a pick sharpener who was in a shed on the pit hill when he heard 'a great crashing' above his head. Entering the engine house, White came across 'the prisoner' [Beresford] who told him that something had struck him on the head and stunned him when the cage was 150 yards from the top of the shaft. Cross-examined, White said that Beresford was 'perfectly sober'. Another witness, John Middleton Gardner who was engineer at Houghton stated that all the machinery, boilers and drawing apparatus were 'in perfect order' on the day of the accident. He went into the engine house almost immediately afterwards and found the steam regulator closed and steam brake on 'as though nothing had happened'. He also said that Beresford should – when the cage was halfway up the shaft – have shut off steam and the impetus would carry the cage to the

The granite memorial to the men killed in the Houghton Main disaster, Darfield churchyard. Photo: Brian Elliott

top. The rope had gone seven revolutions more round the drum than it ought to have done. Cross-examined, Gardner saw no reason not to believe Beresford's statement even though he had never seen splinters of wood knocked from the roof of the engine house which might have been due to the oscillation of the rope. If knocked back by the impact Beresford, holding the levers, would have let the steam in and the accident could then have occurred. Beresford was 'quite sober' in his opinion and was of a good character.

Beresford's sobriety, however, was under further scrutiny. Frederick Baxter, from Darfield, said that he was with the prisoner in three public houses in Wombwell from 11.30 am to 3 pm 'on the day in question'. Cross-examined, Baxter stated that Beresford had had only two glasses of beer and, when he left him, was 'quite sober'. James Henry

An early photograph, c.1905, of Houghton Main. Chris Sharp collection/Old Barnsley

Hall, trammer, described how he met Beresford at 3 pm who then seemed 'worse for drink' and stumbled. However, under cross-examination, Hall said that there was a lot of snow and ice on the ground, so the prisoner may have slipped on ice. There was laughter in the courtroom.

The defence's barrister, Mr Mellor, addressed the jury and said that the prosecution's case was 'of a wretched and shocking character', especially the attempt to show that the prisoner was drunk. He was of the opinion that it was because of prejudice that the learned counsel for the prosecution had tried this ploy. The accident, according to Mellor, was entirely due to overwinding and the question still remained as to how this occurred. Beresford, struck on the head and stunned, made the case for overwinding accounted for.

John Scott Elliott, the certified colliery manager, bore testimony to the excellent character of Beresford and stated that he was sober at the time of the accident. Another man, John Parks, confirmed the engine man's sobriety and that shortly after the accident he did have a bruise on his forehead. Parks also stated that he had often seen pieces of wood fly off the edges of the rope holes. Finally, John Taylor and Samuel Ellis gave further evidence on the good character of Beresford and that he was sober on the day of the accident.

In his summary, Judge Day said that in his opinion the question of 'the gravity of the negligence' was not an issue in this case. Furthermore, if Beresford's evidence was correct he could not have been able to turn the steam off or reverse the levers.

The jury considered their verdict and found Beresford 'not guilty' and he was immediately discharged. The 'cheers' in the room were immediately suppressed in order to maintain the dignity of the occasion.

The victims of the Houghton Main cage disaster were:

Joseph Walker, aged 49, collier, Darfield Bridge, widower, with family
Samuel Walker, 20, trammer, son of the above
Charles Walker, 19, trammer, another son of Joseph Walker
James Hardcastle, 49, collier, Snape Hill, widow and family
Alvin Hardcastle, 18, trammer, son of the above
Joseph Pearson, 47, collier, Snape Hill, married
Joseph Pearson, jnr, 20, trammer, son of the above
Edward Baxter, 29, collier, Snape Hill, single
William Mannion, 40, trammer, Snape Hill
William Barton, 17, pony driver, Snape Bridge

All the men were said to have subscribed to the West Riding Miners' Permanent Relief Fund.

Houghton Main, then owned by the Houghton Main Colliery Company, continued to function as a Barnsley area pit until closure in 1993. Despite protests, all its surface buildings were demolished and the site virtually obliterated from the local landscape. However, the cage disaster has not been forgotten. In 1986, on its one-hundredth anniversary a memorial service was held in Darfield Parish Church and wreaths were laid at the granite monument in the churchyard. Today, aspects of Darfield and district's mining and social history can be seen in the village museum, courtesy of the Darfield Area Amenity Society.

Part Seven

Monuments, Memorials and Mementoes

In the grave where tyrants thrust them,
lies their labour and their pain,
But undying from their sorrow
springeth up hope again.

William Morris

The Gloria Victis *monument shortly after its official opening in 1913.*
Author's collection

Detail of Gloria Victis. *The main element is of a bronze winged female figure in classical garb wearing a stained bronze breast plate. She carries a wounded or dying naked man over her left shoulder as she strides forward. The man hold a broken sword in his right hand. An owl stands by the left foot of the woman. The monument's architects were Wade and Turner, a local firm. The sculptor of the* Gloria Victis *was a Frenchman, MJA Mercie.*
Photo: Brian Elliott

Detail showing the bronze plaque placed under the Gloria Victis *statue.* Photo: Brian Elliott

Several contemporary monuments survive, commemorating the larger pit disasters. Probably the most famous is *Gloria Victis*, the 'Oaks Disaster' monument overlooking Kendray Hill, Barnsley. Placed there in 1913, this spectacular memorial really commemorates the bravery of Parkin Jeffcock and other rescue workers who were killed in the 1866 disaster. Not far away, in Ardsley churchyard, is a memorial dedicated to all the miners who were killed in the Oaks on that dreadful December day.

There are few more tragic reminders of our mining heritage than the Huskar obelisk in Silkstone churchyard and a modern, very moving tribute to the same disaster in Nabs Wood.

Anyone walking in the many churchyards and cemeteries located in the former mining communities of South Yorkshire will find numerous examples of gravestones dedicated to individuals killed in pit accidents and disasters. Some are long forgotten, others still visited. However, for many, including some of my own ancestors, there was little or no money for a stone memorial to mark a loved one killed in a coal mine.

As we have seen, the bodies of many miners were never recovered from the underground workings, a situation that must have meant terrible heartbreak for the bereaved families. Thankfully a great deal of work has been done by members of Family History Societies and History Groups to record details of burials from original records and these are widely available in printed forms, on cd-roms and on the internet. For those of us with mining ancestry, Ian Winstanley's huge national data-base of miners killed in accidents and disasters is well worth accessing (see Bibliography).

For some of the disasters there is no public memorial and most of the old pit sites have

The Huskar disaster memorial in its churchyard setting at Silkstone. Photo: Brian Elliott

long gone, obliterated from the local landscape. But in recent years many individuals and organisations have made a great deal of effort to mark mining deaths by means of commemorative pit wheels. Recent examples can be seen at Armthorpe, Grimethorpe and Thurnscoe. In 2006 a packed church at Goldthorpe witnessed the commemoration of a stained glass memorial window and memorial book in honour of those killed in local collieries. Rachel Horne's 'Out of Darkness Light Project' leads a campaign to get the Ordnance Survey to record pit and other important industrial sites on a National Heritage Map. The well-known Barnsley sculptor Graham Ibbeson has produced some superb public works of art in tribute to Yorkshire and Nottinghamshire miners and mining families. His recent commissions, at Hucknall and South Kirkby are well worth seeing, very moving and much appreciated by their respective communities. A memorial garden, including a distinctive mining feature will soon appear by the side of Barnsley Town Hall.

Much still needs to be done in gratitude to the many hundreds who lost their lives in South Yorkshire accidents and disasters. Like Great War victims we should remember them.

Detail of a mining family monument, a commission by the well-known Barnsley-based sculptor Graham Ibbeson, located outside the NUM headquarters, Barnsley. Photo: Brian Elliott

Detail of a boy miner (left) and a girl miner, Huskar memorial, Nabs Wood. Photo: Brian Elliott

House Carr Lane, Silkstone Common. Near the stream under the bridge is The Huskar Stone, a carved stone monument commissioned by the Silkstone Heritage Stones Project in 1989. Nearby is the site of House Carr Colliery, another one of Clarke's pits. Photo: Brian Elliott

The Huskar Stone. Photo: Brian Elliott

Detail from the Oaks Monument, Ardsley churchyard. Photo: Brian Elliott

"BOAST NOT THYSELF OF
TO MORROW, FOR THOU
KNOWEST NOT WHAT A
DAY MAY BRING FORTH"

Darfield church and part of the Lundhill disaster monument. Photo: Brian Elliott

Several commemorative pottery items were hurriedly produced following the Oaks disaster. This large jug has a transfer print showing the second explosion and is part of the mining memorabilia collection of Frank Burgin. Photo: Brian Elliott

Frank Burgin displays an Oaks mug from his mining collection. Photo: Brian Elliott

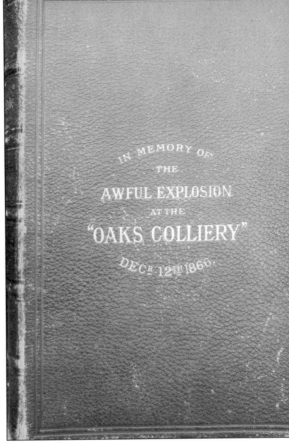

Above, left: *Former Upton colliery miner Kenneth Hammond displays an example of an Oaks Bible, a family heirloom. Photo: Brian Elliott*

Above, right: *Front cover of an Oaks Bible. Photo: Brian Elliott*

Below: *Inscription inside an Oaks Bible presented to Charles Moses Hutchinson in memory of his father who was killed in the disaster. Photo: Brian Elliott*

The Gift of the Oaks Colliery Explosion Subscription Relief Fund Committee, to

Charles Moses Hutchinson

Born *May 22nd 1867*

In Memory of

The terrible Explosion at the Oaks Colliery, near Barnsley, on WEDNESDAY the 12th DECEMBER, 1866, in which *his* Father, and 359 others, men and boys, lost their lives.

President.—THE RIGHT HON. EARL FITZWILLIAM, K.G.

Treasurer.—RICHARD INNS, Esq.

Secretary.—MR. GEO. WM. ATKINSON.

SEARCH THE SCRIPTURES.—*John* v. 39. THEREFORE BE YE ALSO READY.—*Matt.* XXIV. 44.

A pair of Swaithe Main commemorative plates. A coal owner's (Joseph Mitchell) and a Union (J Normanson) version was produced. Photo: Brian Elliott

Detail from a modern commemorative Swaithe Main disaster plate. Photo: Brian Elliott

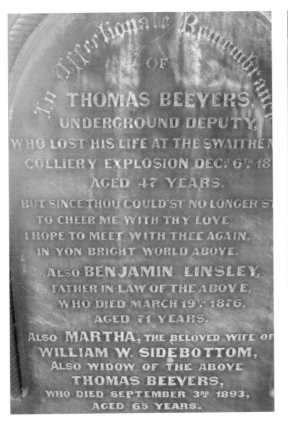

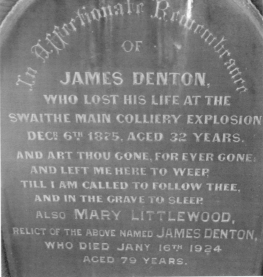

In Affectionate Remembrance
OF
THOMAS BEEVERS,
UNDERGROUND DEPUTY,
WHO LOST HIS LIFE AT THE SWAITHE MAIN
COLLIERY EXPLOSION DECr 6TH 18
AGED 47 YEARS.
BUT SINCE THOU COULD'ST NO LONGER ST
TO CHEER ME WITH THY LOVE,
I HOPE TO MEET WITH THEE AGAIN,
IN YON BRIGHT WORLD ABOVE.
ALSO BENJAMIN LINSLEY,
FATHER IN LAW OF THE ABOVE,
WHO DIED MARCH 19TH 1876,
AGED 71 YEARS.
ALSO MARTHA, THE BELOVED WIFE OF
WILLIAM W. SIDEBOTTOM,
ALSO WIDOW OF THE ABOVE
THOMAS BEEVERS,
WHO DIED SEPTEMBER 3RD 1893,
AGED 65 YEARS.

In Affectionate Remembrance
OF
JAMES DENTON,
WHO LOST HIS LIFE AT THE
SWAITHE MAIN COLLIERY EXPLOSION
DECr 6TH 1875, AGED 32 YEARS.
AND ART THOU GONE, FOR EVER GONE,
AND LEFT ME HERE TO WEEP,
TILL I AM CALLED TO FOLLOW THEE,
AND IN THE GRAVE TO SLEEP.
ALSO MARY LITTLEWOOD,
RELICT OF THE ABOVE NAMED JAMES DENTON,
WHO DIED JANY 16TH 1924
AGED 79 YEARS.

Above: *FOREVER GONE: Gravestone of James Denton who died in the Swaithe Main disaster, aged 32.* Photo: Brian Elliott

Left: *Gravestone of Thomas Beevers, a pit deputy who was killed in the Swaithe disaster of 1875, aged 47.* Photo: Brian Elliott

Below: *Barnsley Main engine house, headstocks and pulley wheel survive as a monument to coal mining in the Barnsley area. Not far from this site but lost underground are the remains of over 80 men and boys who lost their lives in the Oaks colliery on that grim December day in 1866.* Photo: Brian Elliott

FIREDAMP! The name generated fear among miners. Here it is inscribed on the Barnby Furnace monument to the disaster of 1805, probably its earliest reference in stone in South Yorkshire. Photo: Brian Elliott

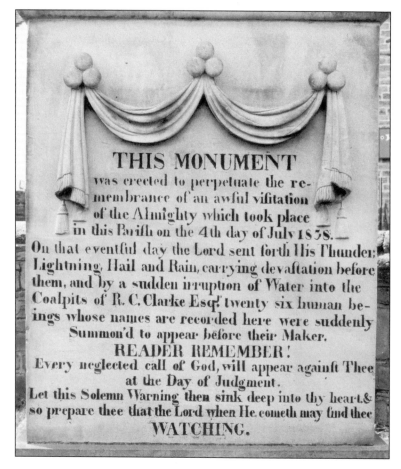

THIS MONUMENT
was erected to perpetuate the remembrance of an awful visitation
of the Almighty which took place
in this Parish on the 4th day of July 1838.
On that eventful day the Lord sent forth His Thunder,
Lightning, Hail and Rain, carrying devastation before
them, and by a sudden irruption of Water into the
Coalpits of R. C. Clarke Esq.' twenty six human be-
ings whose names are recorded here were suddenly
Summon'd to appear before their Maker.
READER REMEMBER!
Every neglected call of God, will appear against Thee
at the Day of Judgment.
Let this Solemn Warning then sink deep into thy heart.&
so prepare thee that the Lord when He cometh may find thee
WATCHING.

Detail from the main inscription on the Huskar disaster monument, Silkstone churchyard. Photo: Brian Elliott

168

Glossary of Mining Terms

adit	a near horizontal entrance to a mine, often used for drainage but also for ventilation and transport.
afterdamp	a mixture of non-inflammable gases left after a 'methane explosion' in a coal mine. Afterdamp often killed more miners than those fatally burnt or maimed in explosions.
bank	the colliery surface, especially around the pit's headgear.
banksman	a person in charge of the shaft and cage or 'skip' at the surface of a colliery. Also see engineman.
blackdamp	see chokedamp.
blackleg	a person who continues to work during a dispute or strike.
box-hole	underground office located near the pit bottom.
brattice	a sheet used for covering ventilation doors and directing air flow. Made of hessian.
brig	headgear.
cage	a timber or metal compartment consisting of 1–3 decks or platforms into which men and/or materials are contained prior to descending/ascending a shaft.
chokedamp	a mine gas consisting of carbon dioxide and nitrogen, usually found in sumps and at floor level. It would put out a lamp flame. Also known as blackdamp. No colour or odour.
Clanny	a type of safety lamp, especially in Northern Coalfields.
coalface	that part of the mine where coal from a seam or bed is extracted.
coalmaster	a person who owns one or more coal mines for a commercial purpose.
collier	a skilled miner who extracts the coal 'hand-got' at the face using a pick, wedges etc. Also known as a 'hewer'.
corve	also 'corf', originally wicker containers for coal, later a general name for tubs.
cupola	a shaft above an underground furnace.
damp	an old name for mine gas.
Davy	a safety lamp of the type invented by Sir Humphrey Davy in 1815.
day-hole	a surface drift mine, usually not extensive.
deputy	an official responsible for safety and the day-to-day deployment of men.
dip	angle/slope of rock strata/coal seam or drift.

district	underground area of a mine where particular coal seams are worked; usually a named area.
downcast	shaft through which fresh air enters the mine.
draw	upward or downward movement of the cage.
drift	entrance tunnel into a mine, driven through rock strata/hillside to reach the coal (cf vertical shaft) or an incline or heading made from one part of the underground workings to another.
engineman	person employed to operate the winding apparatus in an engine house.
explosions	the ignition of combustible firedamp gas (a mixture of methane [principally], carbon monoxide, nitrogen, ethane, carbon dioxide) and air. The range is between 5.4% and 14.8%. A very serious explosion is one involving coal dust, caused by fine dust particles being ignited in dry workings. This could be a result of shot-firing or the spreading of a minor explosion blast wave, creating a dust cloud which is then ignited by the initial flame of the explosion.
face	see coalface.
firedamp	explosive gas (in certain quantities) released from coal seams, the origin of many colliery explosions.
fire-trier	in Victorian times a miner responsible for testing for gas in old and current workings and giving the 'all- clear', warnings etc; a dangerous job as naked lights were often used.
furnace	see ventilating furnace.
gate	underground roadway or tunnel.
goaf	area for waste; worked out area; potentially dangerous place where gas might accumulate.
gob	another name for goaf.
haulage hand	a person employed underground or at the surface in regard to the conveyance of coal, equipment or materials; also in the turning of coal tubs at a junction or uncoupling chains from the haulage rope.
headgear	timber frame with pulley wheels placed over a shaft.
hewer	see collier.
hooker-on	a haulage hand employed underground who attached the coal tubs/corves onto a moving haulage rope.
Hoppet	a large bucket attached to the winding rope at a shaft, usually used in pit sinking operations but also for emergency access up and down a shaft when the cage was out of service/broken.
horsekeeper	person in charge of pit ponies and horses.
hurrier	see trammer.
jinny	an incline.

laik	Yorkshire dialect word meaning to play or take time off work.
level	a horizontal drivage tunnel following the course of a seam of coal.
lock-out	a colliery closed by the owner during a dispute, usually a ploy to get the men back on his or the company's terms.
longwall	a system of working coal involving several men working along a coal-face and where pillars are not used, the roof allowed to fall behind the line of supports.
Main	a term, almost peculiar to Yorkshire, added to the name of a colliery if its principal seam was from the famous Barnsley bed of coal.
maingate	the main roadway leading to (or from) each mining district or coalface from the pit bottom.
methane	a colourless and odourless gas which forms an explosive mixture when in contact with air.
naked light	a lit candle or other exposed flames, for example in an oil lamp. Often the cause of explosions.
ostler	see horsekeeper.
overwinding	when a cage is drawn up too high, sometimes with disastrous consequences.
pit bank	main surface area of the mine, especially around the headgear.
pit-bottom	area at and close to the bottom of the shaft where there is access to the cage; often a cold place to work.
pit hill	see pit bank.
pony driver	a young person in charge of a pit pony or horse, employed in the haulage of coal and materials underground.
prop	roof support, usually of timber in the Victorian period.
roadway	underground passage or tunnel to reach working areas and through which ventilation passes.
safety lamp	a form of lighting which is safe to be used underground, the flame protected from igniting any inflammable gases by gauzes and glass. Early makes included Davy, Stephenson and Clanny.
seam	a layer, bed or strata of coal, usually given the name relevant to its geological or geographic origin; and also its width eg Thin, Thick.
shaft	a vertical hole usually circular, sunk from the surface to reach one or more seams of coal.
shift	period of work, usually day (morning), afternoon or night.
shot	explosive charge, usually by gunpowder.
shot-firer	person who uses explosives in stone drifts and coal workings.
slit	a narrow underground passageway used, for example, in an emergency.

stableman	see horsekeeper.
Stephenson	a type of safety lamp invented by the great pioneer of steam locomotion, George Stephenson in 1815. He was the son of a fireman at a Northumbrian colliery.
steward	an experienced man employed by a colliery owner in regard to the safe and efficient operation of the mine above and/or below ground. A day-to-day representative of the owner(s).
sump	an extension of the pit shaft in the pit bottom containing water that has seeped downwards.
tippler	a mechanical device used to empty tubs of coal.
trammer	a miner, often a young man, who pushes wheeled tubs or corves on rails to and from the workings; often employed by the collier. Known as a 'drawer' in Lancs.
trapper	a solitary job; a young boy (or before 1842 a girl) assigned to open and close ventilation doors as and when required; often worked with little or no light.
upcast	the ventilation shaft that carries foul air away, assisted by an underground furnace or fan.
ventilating fan	mechanical means of extracting air from the mine via the upcast shaft.
ventilating furnace	An early form of mine ventilation whereby a furnace (in the form of a controlled fire) was placed at the bottom of a shaft, and drawing cleaner and fresher air into the workings via another shaft.
viewer	Victorian term for a manager/under-manager at a colliery.
winder	see engineman.

Select bibliography

Books

Atkinson, F. *The Great Northern Coalfield 1700–1900* (London, University Tutorial Press, 1968)

Baylies, C. *The History of the Yorkshire Miners 1881–1918* (London & New York, Routledge, 1993)

Benson, J. *British Coalminers in the Nineteenth Century: A Social History* (New York, Holmes & Meier, 1980)

Benson, J. & Neville, R.G. (eds). *Studies in the Yorkshire Coal Industry* (Manchester, MUP, 1976)

Brearley, G. *Grave Tales of South Yorkshire* (Barnsley, Wharncliffe, 2000)

Burton, A. *The Miners* (London, Futura, 1977)

Cynon Valley Historical Society. *Cynon Coal* (Cynon, 2001)

Duckham, H. & B. *Great Pit Disasters* (Newton Abbot, David & Charles, 1973)

Elliott, B. *Pits and Pitmen of Barnsley* (Barnsley, Wharncliffe, 2001)

Elliott, B. *The Making of Barnsley* (Barnsley, Wharncliffe, 1988, 2004)

Elliott, B. *Yorkshire Miners* (Stroud, Sutton, 2004)

Gallop, A. *Children of the Dark* (Stroud, Sutton, 2003)

Goodchild, J. *Coals From Barnsley* (Barnsley, Wakefield Historical Publications, 1986)

Goodchild, J. *South Yorkshire Collieries* (Stroud, Tempus, 2001)

Gorman, J. *To Build Jerusalem* (London, Scorpion, 1980)

Hey, D. *A History of Yorkshire* (Lancaster, Carnegie, 2005)

Jackson, B. *Cawthorne 1790–1990* (Cawthorne, Cawthorne Victoria Museum, 1991)

Machin, F. *The Yorkshire Miners*, Volume 1 (Barnsley, NUM, 1958)

Nadin, J. *Lancashire Mining Disasters 1835–1910* (Barnsley, Wharncliffe Books, 2006)

Pollard, M. *The Hardest Work Under Heaven* (London, Hutchinson, 1984)

Pratt, Rev. C. T. *History of Cawthorne* (Barnsley, privately printed, 1882)

Prince, Rev. J. *The History and Topography of the Parish of Silkstone in the County of York* (Penistone, J.H.Wood, 1922)

Royston Pike, E. *Human Documents of the Industrial Revolution in Britain* (London, George Allen & Unwin, 1966)

Sykes, G. N. *Silkstone Ancient and Modern* (Huddersfield, West Riding Duplicating Company, 1976)

Thornes, R. *Images of Industry. Coal* (Swindon, RCHME, 1994)

Threlkeld, J. *Pits. A Pictorial Record of Mining in Barnsley* (Barnsley, Wharncliffe, 1987)

Threlkeld, J. *Pits 2. A Pictorial Record of Mining* (Barnsley, Wharncliffe, 1989)

Williams, P. *Images of Yorkshire Coal* (Ashbourne, Landmark, 2005)

Withington, J. *A Disastrous History of Britain* (Stroud, Sutton Publishing Ltd, 2005)

Wood, J. *To Commemorate the Huskar Pit Disaster* (Silkstone, privately printed, 1988)

Articles/Reports

Goodchild, J. 'The Silkstone Railway' in Elliott, B. (ed). *Aspects of Barnsley 2* (Barnsley, Wharncliffe, 1994)

Goodchild, J. 'Up Wakefield Road' in Elliott, B. (ed). *Aspects of Barnsley 5* (Barnsley, Wharncliffe, 1998)

'Ingleton Coalfield', British Mining No. 76, Northern Mine Research Society.

Jones, M. 'Child Labour in Mines in the Barnsley Area in the Early Victorian period: Evidence from the Children's Employment Commission' in Elliott, B. (ed). *Aspects of Barnsley 4* (Barnsley, Wharncliffe, 1996)

(Annual) Reports of H.M. Inspectors of Mines

Newspapers & Magazines

Barnsley Chronicle

Barnsley Record

Barnsley Times

Colliery Guardian

Doncaster Chronicle

Illustrated London News

Leeds Intelligencer

Leeds Mercury

London Telegraph

Sheffield Iris

Sheffield & Rotherham Independent

South Yorkshire Times

The Times

Wakefield Journal

York Courant

Unpublished

Elliott, B. *Explosions in Coal Mines. The Tragedy of the Oaks Colliery* (B.Ed dissertation, Matlock College [University of Nottingham], 1969

Hawley, G. *Incidents, Accidents & Disasters – Silkstone and Dodworth Collieries*